DATE DUE

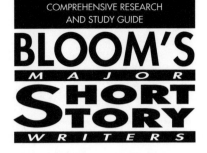

COMPREHENSIVE RESEARCH
AND STUDY GUIDE

BLOOM'S
MAJOR
SHORT
STORY
WRITERS

Nathaniel

Hawthorne

EDITED AND WITH AN
INTRODUCTION BY HAROLD BLOOM

COMPREHENSIVE RESEARCH
AND STUDY GUIDE

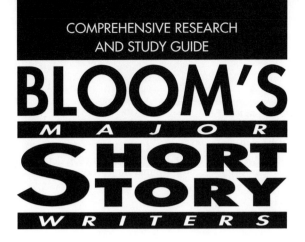

BLOOM'S *MAJOR* **SHORT STORY** *WRITERS*

Nathaniel Hawthorne

EDITED AND

BLOOM

3 5 7 9 8 6 4 2

Library of Congress Cataloging-in-Publication Data
Nathaniel Hawthorne / edited by Harold Bloom.
         p. cm. — (Bloom's major short story writers)
     Includes bibliographical references and index.
     ISBN 0-7910-5949-9 (alk. paper)
     1. Hawthorne, Nathaniel, 1804–1864—Criticism and interpretation
—Handbooks, manuals, etc. 2. Hawthorne, Nathaniel, 1804–
1864—Examinations—Study guides. 3. Short story—Examinations
—Study guides. 4. Short story—Handbooks, manuals, etc.
I. Bloom, Harold. II. Series.
PS1888.N295   2000
813'.3—dc21   00-055587
                                                      CIP

Chelsea House Publishers
1974 Sproul Road, Suite 400
Broomall, PA 19008-0914

The Chelsea House World Wide Web address is
http://www.chelseahouse.com

Contributing Editor: Aaron Tillman

Produced by: Robert Gerson Publisher's Services, Santa Barbara, CA

Contents

User's Guide

This volume is designed to present biographical, critical, and bibliographical information on the author's best-known or most important short stories. Following Harold Bloom's editor's note and introduction is a detailed biography of the author, discussing major life events and important literary accomplishments. A plot summary of each short story follows, tracing significant themes, patterns, and motifs in the work, and an annotated list of characters supplies brief information on the main characters in each story.

A selection of critical extracts, derived from previously published material from leading critics, analyzes aspects of each short story. The extracts consist of statements from the author, if available, early reviews of the work, and later evaluations up to the present. A bibliography of the author's writings (including a complete list of all books written, cowritten, edited, and translated), a list of additional books and articles on the author and the work, and an index of themes and ideas in the author's writings conclude the volume.

~

Harold Bloom is Sterling Professor of the Humanities at Yale University and Henry W. and Albert A. Berg Professor of English at the New York University Graduate School. He is the author of over 20 books, including *Shelley's Mythmaking* (1959), *The Visionary Company* (1961), *Blake's Apocalypse* (1963), *Yeats* (1970), *A Map of Misreading* (1975), *Kabbalah and Criticism* (1975), *Agon: Toward a Theory of Revisionism* (1982), *The American Religion* (1992), *The Western Canon* (1994), and *Omens of Millennium: The Gnosis of Angels, Dreams, and Resurrection* (1996). *The Anxiety of Influence* (1973) sets forth Professor Bloom's provocative theory of the literary relationships between the great writers and their predecessors. His most recent books include *Shakespeare: The Invention of the Human,* a 1998 National Book Award finalist, and *How to Read and Why,* which was published in 2000.

Professor Bloom earned his Ph.D. from Yale University in 1955 and has served on the Yale faculty since then. He is a 1985 MacArthur Foundation Award recipient, served as the Charles Eliot Norton Professor of Poetry at Harvard University in 1987–88, and has received honorary degrees from the universities of Rome and Bologna. In 1999, Professor Bloom received the prestigious American Academy of Arts and Letters Gold Medal for Criticism.

Currently, Harold Bloom is the editor of numerous Chelsea House volumes of literary criticism, including the series BLOOM'S NOTES, BLOOM'S MAJOR DRAMATISTS, BLOOM'S MAJOR NOVELISTS, MAJOR LITERARY CHARACTERS, MODERN CRITICAL VIEWS, MODERN CRITICAL INTERPRETATIONS, and WOMEN WRITERS OF ENGLISH AND THEIR WORKS.

Editor's Note

My Introduction adds "Feathertop," Hawthorne's late masterpiece, to the five more famous stories discussed in this volume. "Feathertop" is the essence of Hawthorne's art as a story-writer, and casts a final illumination upon "Young Goodman Brown," "The Minister's Black Veil," "The Maypole of Merry Mount," "Rappaccini's Daughter," and "Roger Malvin's Burial."

All twenty-six of the Critical Views excerpted here have considerable usefulness, and I will note only a few that have influenced me. These include Henry James, our greatest novelist, on "Young Goodman Brown," and Richard H. Brodhead on "The Minister's Black Veil."

"The Maypole of Merry Mount" found its classical commentator in the late Harry Levin, while Ann Brickhouse provides a surprising new perspective upon "Rappaccini's Daughter."

Michael J. Colacurcio sets "Roger Malvin's Burial" in historical context, with rare and incisive authority.

Introduction

HAROLD BLOOM

My personal favorite among all of Hawthorne's tales is "Feathertop," subtitled "A Moralized Legend." The great witch Mother Rigby creates a scarecrow; like Jehovah, she looks on her work and is pleased. A New Adam therefore is made, and is breathed into life, as Jehovah did Adam, though Mother Rigby prefers to do the job by sharing a pipe-puffing with her creature. Feathertop, as she names him, can survive only by puffing away.

Attired in some finery, Feathertop is sent out by his witch-mother to woo and win the pretty Polly Gookin, daughter of a town worthy much indebted to the witch Rigby. Gookin plainly sees that Feathertop is unreal, but is too afraid of Mother Rigby to intervene.

Poor Polly falls in love with the animated scarecrow, and passion portends, when alas both she and Feathertop glance at themselves in a mirror. Polly faints and Feathertop rushes back to Mother Rigby, for the mirror reveals his sordid reality and prompts Hawthorne to a wonderfully mordant reflection:

> For perchance the only time, since this so often and deceptive life of mortals began its course, an Illusion had seen and fully recognized itself.

Jorge Luis Borges, who was deeply influenced by Hawthorne's tales, could not have bettered the irony of the resolution. Feathertop, who has seen the truth, cannot survive it:

> "I've seen myself, mother!—I've seen myself for the wretched, ragged, empty thing I am!"

Feathertop, an idealistic scarecrow, is no King Lear, who also sees himself as the bare forked thing a man is, wretched, ragged, and naked to the heavens. Yet Lear, every inch a king, battles on to the end. Feathertop immolates himself. The amiable Mother Rigby has the last word, knowing that her child had feelings too tender, sensibilities too deep for a heartless world. Feathertop, the American Adam, subsides into a scarecrow. ❀

Biography of
Nathaniel Hawthorne

Nathaniel Hawthorne was born on July 4, 1804, the only son and second child of Nathaniel and Elizabeth Manning Hathorne (he added the "w" to his name as an adult). Four years after his birth, Nathaniel's father, a sea captain, died of yellow fever in Suriname, Dutch Guiana. Following his death, Elizabeth Manning Hathorne took Nathaniel and his two sisters, Elisabeth and Louisa, to live with the Manning family in Salem, Massachusetts.

In 1818 the Hathorne family moved to Raymond, Maine, where the Mannings owned a home. The following year, Nathaniel returned to Salem and attended Samuel Archer's school. Two years later, after being tutored by Benjamin L. Oliver, he enrolled at Bowdoin College in Brunswick, Maine, where he spent the next four years. His classmates included the writer Henry Wadsworth Longfellow and Franklin Pierce, the future president of the United States, who became one of Hawthorne's closest friends.

After graduating from Bowdoin, Hawthorne returned to Salem, where he lived quietly in his mother's house. He polished his writing skills by penning tales and sketches and generating ideas for poems and stories. In 1828, he published his first novel, *Fanshawe: A Tale*, anonymously and at his own expense. Hawthorne was disappointed with the finished work, however, and he recalled and burned nearly all of the copies.

During the next few years, Hawthorne published a number of tales and sketches in various literary journals including *The Token* and *The Salem Gazette*. In 1836, he moved to Boston to edit *The American Magazine of Useful and Entertaining Knowledge.* He also worked as an editor, along with his sister, on *Peter Parley's Universal History on the Basis of Geography.* In March 1837, his collection of short stories and sketches, *Twice-Told Tales*, was published.

In November 1837, Hawthorne met Sophia Peabody, and they were engaged in 1838. Hawthorne realized that his earnings from writing would not be enough to support the two of them when they were married. He asked for, and received, an appointment to a government job as an inspector in the Boston Custom House. The job paid well but involved long hours, which made it difficult to find time to write. Hawthorne did publish a book of historical stories for children called *Grandfather's Chair*, as well as the works *Famous Old People* and *Liberty Tree*.

After two years at the Custom House, Hawthorne left to live at Brook Farm, an experimental Utopian community based on Transcendentalist and Socialist philosophy. He left the Farm for the same reason he had left the Custom House: he found it too difficult to write.

On July 9, 1842, not long after the second edition of *Twice-Told Tales* appeared, Nathaniel Hawthorne and Sophia Peabody were married. They moved to the Old Manse in Concord, Massachusetts, where he began writing regularly. On March 3, 1844, their first child, Una, was born. The following year, after financial problems forced them to move in with his mother and sisters in Salem, he worked as an editor on Horatio Bridge's *Journal of an African Cruiser*. On July 22, 1846, Nathaniel and Sophia's son Julian was born. During that same year, the short story collection *Mosses from an Old Manse* was published.

In July 1849, Nathaniel's mother died. Later that summer he began writing *The Scarlet Letter*, which was published in March 1850. In May of that year, the Hawthornes moved to Lenox, Massachusetts. He met Herman Melville in August. They became close and Melville dedicated *Moby-Dick* to him the following year. In 1851 Hawthorne published another novel, *The House of the Seven Gables*, as well as *The Snow-Image and Other Twice-Told Tales* and *True Stories from History and Biography*.

In 1852, Hawthorne published *The Blithedale Romance*, a children's book called *A Wonder-Book for Girls and Boys*, and *The Life of Franklin Pierce*, a biography of his close friend, who was running for president. In 1853 he published *Tanglewood Tales*, classical myths for children. Later that year, the Hawthornes sailed to Liverpool where Nathaniel served as United States consul at Liverpool, having been appointed by his friend, President Franklin Pierce.

In 1854, a revised edition of *Mosses from an Old Manse* was published. In 1857, Hawthorne and his family moved to France and later to Rome and Florence, Italy, where they stayed until their return to England on June 24, 1859. In 1860, Hawthorne's last novel, *The Marble Faun,* was published, and the author returned to Concord, Massachusetts. In 1863 Hawthorne published *Our Old Home,* a collection of sketches about England which was dedicated to Franklin Pierce.

Nathaniel Hawthorne died on May 19, 1864, in Plymouth, New Hampshire. He was buried on May 23 at the Sleepy Hollow Cemetery in Concord, Massachusetts. Four unfinished novels were found among his papers, including *Septimus Felton* (1872) and *The Dolliver Romance* (1876). ❀

Plot Summary of
"Young Goodman Brown"

"Young Goodman Brown," one of Nathaniel Hawthorne's most celebrated tales, opens in Salem village as Goodman Brown is about to leave his young wife of three months, Faith, to go on an overnight errand into the forest. After speaking with his concerned spouse, who begs him not to leave her alone, Goodman Brown departs along the road toward the woods. "He had taken a dreary road, darkened by all the gloomiest trees of the forest, which barely stood aside to let the narrow path creep through, and closed immediately behind."

After passing a crook in the road, Goodman Brown sees the man he expected to meet sitting beside an old tree. This man stands upon seeing young Brown and greets him by name, claiming that he has arrived late. This man resembles an older version of Goodman Brown himself. He is carrying a staff which looks like a long black snake and even seems to "twist and wriggle itself like a living serpent. This, of course must have been an ocular deception, assisted by the uncertain light." They walk together toward the heart of the dark forest before Goodman Brown stops in protest. He says he has fulfilled his obligation to meet the man in the forest, and would now like to turn around, as he is too moral a man to continue. However, the older man convinces him to continue walking.

Goodman Brown says that he is from a family of honest, good Christian men who would never agree to walk this path. The older man counters by saying that he is quite familiar with the Brown family: he helped Goodman Brown's grandfather when he had "lashed the Quaker woman," and handed his father a torch to "set fire to an Indian village." He goes on to say that he has walked this path and shared significant experiences with many people throughout New England, including deacons and members of the General Court and even the governor. Goodman Brown is shocked by these statements, but maintains that even if everything stated is true, he would not be able to handle the guilt inflicted by the eyes of his minister, not to mention his wife.

The older man laughs and points out the approaching woman, Goody Cloyse, who had been Goodman Brown's catechism teacher and remains his spiritual advisor, along with his minister and

Deacon Gookin. Fearful of her judgment, Goodman Brown decides to hide until she has passed. The older man approaches Goody Cloyse and it becomes clear that they are familiar with one another. Goody Cloyse says that she is heading off to see a nice young man who is taking communion that evening. The older man lends her his serpent-like staff and they part ways.

Goodman Brown is shocked by this interaction. He walks a bit further before deciding to stop beside a tree, refusing to move on. He claims that the actions of his spiritual advisor should not force him to follow the same path. The older man gives Goodman Brown a maple staff that he had found and then disappears.

Soon after the older man's disappearance, Goodman Brown hears a carriage riding through the woods. He jumps off the path and crouches behind a tree. He is witness to a conversation between the minister and Deacon Gookin. They are discussing deviltry and their excitement over the goodly young woman who will be taking communion that evening.

Once again Goodman Brown is in a state of disbelief. He wonders if there is a heaven above. He vows to remain good as long as Faith, his wife, is on earth. When he hears a group of voices in the distance, he recognizes some of them from Salem village. He even thinks he hears Faith's voice, and cries out for her. His screams are met by laughter and noise, then a pink ribbon floats through the air and lands in a nearby tree. Goodman Brown seizes the ribbon and discovers that it is the same ribbon that had been tied into Faith's hair when he had left her. "My Faith is gone!" he yells. "There is no good on earth; and sin is but a name. Come, devil; for to thee is this world given." Goodman Brown then laughs wildly and sets off toward the heart of the dark forest. He speeds maniacally past the trees and into the howling wind, laughing all the while and displaying the fierceness of his own despair.

Goodman Brown sees a red light pulsing out of the heart of the forest. There is a congregation of people surrounding this light. He recognizes faces from his town, people who would appear the following day in the congregation of the church. Mingled with the pious are known sinners and Indian priests: "The good shrank not from the wicked, nor were the sinners abashed by the saints."

"But where is Faith?" Goodman Brown wonders, feeling a small sense of hope. Hymns of evil are belted out by the choir as Goodman Brown waits in the darkness surrounding the group. Following a cry for the converts to be brought forth, Goodman Brown steps into the circle of Satan where he is seized by Deacon Gookin and the minister. A dark figure with indiscriminate features begins to recite the various sins of the townsfolk. It is at this point that Faith is brought forth to stand beside her husband, "trembling before that unhallowed alter."

When Goodman Brown and Faith are brought together, the dark figure acknowledges the significance of the moment: "Now are ye undeceived. Evil is the nature of mankind. Evil must be your only happiness. Welcome again, my children, to the communion of your race." Goodman Brown looks at his wife and implores her, "look up to heaven, and resist the wicked one." He does not know if she follows his advice; in the next moment, he wakes up in the middle of the cold woods, alone.

The next morning, Goodman Brown stumbles into Salem village a changed man. He sees the minister, Deacon Gookin, and the rest of the townsfolk going about their usual routine, and recoils from their hidden evil natures that were revealed in the forest. When he finds Goody Cloyse teaching catechism to a little girl, Goodman Brown snatches her away "as from the grasp of the fiend himself." And when Faith catches sight of her husband and rushes happily to greet him, Goodman Brown meets her gaze and walks past without a word.

"Had Goodman Brown fallen asleep in the forest and only dreamed a wild dream of a witch meeting?" asks the narrative. "Be it so, if you will; but alas! it was a dream of evil omen for young Goodman Brown." The narrative concludes by discussing how intolerable the hypocrisies of the townsfolk become for Goodman Brown. He goes on to live a long life, but when he dies, leaving behind his wife, children, grandchildren, "they carved no hopeful verse upon his tombstone; for his dying hour was gloom." ❀

List of Characters in
"Young Goodman Brown"

Goodman Brown is the primary character in the story. He leaves his wife, Faith, on an overnight errand through the forest. After meeting the Devil on a forest path, he becomes tormented about the obscure purpose behind his errand. He sees a number of familiar faces throughout his journey, and is shocked to discover that their true natures are evil. Goodman eventually wanders into a devilish ceremony where he sees Faith, and realizes that the members of the community have gathered for the purpose of watching he and his wife take the sacramental communion of evil. The story ends after Goodman rejects evil, wakes alone in the woods, and returns to town, unable to tolerate the false piousness of the townsfolk.

Faith Brown is the wife of Goodman Brown. She is wearing pink ribbons when he sets out into the woods. Her name and her dress are symbolic of her innocent nature. When Goodman Brown arrives at the meeting in the woods, Faith is already there. Goodman Brown tells her to look heavenward to resist the evil communion, but he never learns whether she followed this exhortation.

The Devil meets Goodman Brown in the woods. He looks something like Goodman Brown himself, and is carrying a cane that looks like a serpent. He tells Goodman that he was with his father and grandfather during their darkest moments. He is conducting the ceremony in the woods that Goodman Brown is fated to find.

Goody Cloyse is one of Goodman's spiritual advisors. She had been his catechism teacher when he was younger. Goodman sees her speaking with the Devil on his walk through the woods.

Deacon Gookin is one of Goodman's spiritual advisors. He is present at the final meeting in the woods.

The Minister is one of Goodman's spiritual advisors. He is present at the final meeting in the woods, and he is composing his sermon when Goodman first walks into town the following morning. ❈

Critical Views on
"Young Goodman Brown"

HENRY JAMES ON IMAGINATION AND ALLEGORY

[Henry James (1843–1916) was a widely acclaimed American novelist. His works include *Daisy Miller, The Portrait of a Lady,* and *The Wings of the Dove.* In this excerpt, James recognizes the imaginative caliber of the story but claims that its tendency toward allegory is its largest fault.]

Hawthorne was a man of fancy, and I suppose that, in speaking of him, it is inevitable that we should feel ourselves confronted with the familiar problem of the difference between the fancy and the imagination. Of the larger and more potent faculty he certainly possessed a liberal share; no one can read *The House of the Seven Gables* without feeling it to be a deeply imaginative work. But I am often struck, especially in the shorter tales, of which I am now chiefly speaking, with a kind of small ingenuity, a taste for conceits and analogies, which bears more particularly what is called the fanciful stamp. The finer of the shorter tales are redolent of a rich imagination.

> "Had Goodman Brown fallen asleep in the forest and only dreamed a wild dream of witch-meeting? Be it so, if you will; but, alas, it was a dream of evil omen for young Goodman Brown! a stern, a sad, a darkly meditative, a distrustful, if not a desperate, man, did he become from the night of that fearful dream. On the Sabbath-day, when the congregation were singing a holy psalm, he could not listen, because an anthem of sin rushed loudly upon his ear and drowned all the blessed strain. When the minister spoke from the pulpit, with power and fervid eloquence, and with his hand on the open Bible of the sacred truth of our religion, and of saint-like lives and triumphant deaths, and of future bliss or misery unutterable, then did Goodman Brown grow pale, dreading lest the roof should thunder down upon the gray blasphemer and his hearers. Often, awaking suddenly at midnight, he shrank from the bosom of Faith; and at morning or eventide, when the family knelt down at prayer, he scowled and muttered to himself, and gazed sternly at his wife, and turned away. And when he had lived long, and was borne to his grave a hoary corpse, followed by Faith, an aged woman, and children, and grandchildren, a goodly procession, besides neighbours not a few, they carved no hopeful verse upon his tombstone, for his dying hour was gloom."

There is imagination in that, and in many another passage that I might quote; but as a general thing I should characterise the more metaphysical of our author's short stories as graceful and felicitous conceits. They seem to me to be qualified in this manner by the very fact that they belong to the province of allegory. Hawthorne, in his metaphysical moods, is nothing if not allegorical, and allegory, to my sense, is quite one of the lighter exercises of the imagination. Many excellent judges, I know, have a great stomach for it; they delight in symbols and correspondences, in seeing a story told as if it were another and a very different story. I frankly confess that I have, as a general thing, but little enjoyment of it, and that it has never seemed to me to be, as it were, a first-rate literary form.

—Henry James, *Hawthorne* (Ithaca, N.Y.: Cornell University Press, 1966): pp. 48–50.

DARREL ABEL ON THE PINK RIBBON AS SYMBOL

[Darrel Abel was a professor at Purdue University for thirty years. He edited *American Literature: Critical Theory in the American Renaissance*. In this excerpt, Abel discusses the importance of the pink ribbon in the middle of the story.]

In the midscene of "Young Goodman Brown" the young goodman, after a succession of dismaying assaults by the Devil upon his naive belief in human goodness, "fancied" that he heard the voice of his wife Faith in the midst of a black cloud filled with a "confused and doubtful sound of voices." He shouted her name "in a voice of agony and desperation"; then, as the dark cloud swept away, "something fluttered lightly down through the air and caught on the branch of a tree. The young man seized it and beheld a pink ribbon." Recognizing it as belonging to his wife Faith, "after one stupefied moment," he cried out, "My faith is gone! . . . There is no good on earth; and sin is but a name. Come, Devil; for to thee is this world given."

This obviously crucial incident is loaded with meaning because of the symbolism of the pink ribbon, the circumstances of its discovery and the speech that accompanies its recognition, and the crucial point which the incident illuminates in the narration.

The pink ribbons that adorn the cap which Faith wears on her pretty little head are a badge of feminine innocence, which they inevitably suggest in consequence of the immemorial custom of decking baby girls in pink ribbons. Faith's pink ribbons worn in the daylight of the Puritan village show her to be an innocent dwelling in the midst of innocence. But detached from this ensemble of purity, and found "in the heart of the dark wilderness" into which Satan beguiles the innocent, the pink ribbon becomes part of "a design of darkness to appall."

It is no longer the unshaken first premise of the young goodman that the Puritan community is godly, or even that the most apparently innocent person is good. The defenses of example, custom, and fear that his Preventing God has set around him do not suffice to keep him from gauging the depths of sin to which human nature may descend. The young man has the vulnerability of youth and, having newly yielded to the persuasions of the Devil, he has been led step by step to mistrust all he had believed in. Therefore, accepting the indications of the pink ribbon which he beheld on the dark forest path, and "maddened with despair," he rushed headlong into the "benighted wilderness."

This crucial incident occurs in the middle one of three scenes including notice of the pink ribbon that structure the tale. The pink ribbon, like the black glove ⟨from *The Scarlet Letter*⟩, has the function of orienting the visible with the invisible world. When Goodman Brown takes leave of Faith at sunset in the street of Salem Village, the pink ribbons give him visual assurance that she is "a blessed angel on earth." But the author goes speedily to his business of promoting an insurrection in the moral kingdom of Young Goodman Brown. The mysterious "errand" on which the young man "must" go is a figure for the fall from innocence to experience; he was impelled to it by "the instinct that guides mortal man to evil."

—Darrel Abel, *The Moral Picturesque: Studies in Hawthorne's Fiction* (West Lafayette, Ind.: Purdue University Press, 1988): pp. 130–31.

Joan Elizabeth Easterly on Goodman Brown's Spiritual Failure

[Joan Elizabeth Easterly has taught English and Foreign Languages at Pellissippi State Technical Community College in Knoxville. In this excerpt, Easterly discusses Goodman Brown's lack of response to his loss of faith.]

"Faith! Faith!" cried the husband. "Look up to Heaven, and resist the Wicked One!"

Whether Faith obeyed, he knew not. Hardly had he spoken, when he found himself amid calm night and solitude, listening to a roar of the wind, which died heavily away through the forest. He staggered against the rock and felt it chill and damp, while a hanging twig, that had been all on fire, besprinkled his cheek with the coldest dew.

Thus ends the crucial scene in Nathaniel Hawthorne's tale of "Young Goodman Brown," the story of a Puritan lad who leaves his bride of three months to secretly watch a witches' Sabbath in the deep forest outside Salem village. In so doing, he willfully betrays his commitment to his wife, the moral code of his society, and the teachings of his religion. The experience of this one night in the forest changes Goodman Brown for the rest of his life, for it poisons his relationship with his wife, isolates him from his neighbors, and destroys his ability to worship God. Whether dream or reality, one wild night is the turning point of Brown's existence; afterward he is "a stern, a sad, a darkly meditative, a distrustful, if not a desperate man" and, when he dies, "they carved no hopeful verse upon his tombstone."

Literary critics have interpreted the significance of Goodman Brown's experience in many fashions—allegorical, moral, philosophical, and psychological. However, there is an intriguing absence of any reference to the last line of the Sabbath scene to explain Hawthorne's characterization of the young Puritan, despite the fact that Hawthorne signals the importance of the cold drops of dew in a periodic sentence. In essence, Hawthorne here carefully delineates the image of a young man who has faced and failed a critical test of moral and spiritual maturity.

Young Goodman Brown, leaning against the cold rock after the witch-meeting vanishes, is reproached by his creator because he shows no compassion for the weaknesses he sees in others, no remorse for his own sin, and no sorrow for his loss of faith. The one action that would demonstrate such deep and redemptive human feelings does not take place. Goodman Brown does not weep. Therefore, Hawthorne quietly and gently sprinkles "the coldest dew" on his cheek to represent the absence of tears.

This lack of tears, the outward sign of an inward reality, posits the absence of the innate love and humility that would have made possible Brown's moral and spiritual progression. A meticulous artist and a master of symbolism, Hawthorne uses the twig and dewdrops deliberately. Drops of water on a man's cheek can only suggest tears.

The hanging twig that sprinkles the drops of water on Goodman Brown's face calls to mind a picture of the beadle perched on a high stool in the back of a Puritan meeting house, holding two long switches. According to legend, one switch had a feather attached to the end and the other a stone or burr. If a lady fell asleep during the long service, the beadle would awaken her by tickling her face with the feather, but any gentleman inclined to drowse or small boys inclined to mischief knew that the stone hung over their heads like the bait on a long fishing rod and that their recall to propriety would not be so gentle. Likewise, Goodman Brown is awakened to reality from his dream or vision by a "hanging twig" that had been burning during the witch meeting but now scatters cold dew on his cheek. Like the beadle's switch, a twig from on high is the vehicle for bringing to Brown's face the reminder of what would be correct behavior and attitude for a man in this situation. He should be weeping, but he is not.

—Joan Elizabeth Easterly, "Lachrymal Imagery in Hawthorne's 'Young Goodman Brown,'" *Studies in Short Fiction* 28, no. 3 (Summer 1991): pp. 339–40.

[Walter Shear is a professor of English at Pittsburg State University in Kansas. He has written essays on Hawthorne, Washington Irving, Mark Twain, and William Saroyan, amongst others. In this excerpt, Shear discusses time and social fantasy within the story.]

Hawthorne seems, at the beginning, merely to acknowledge social ties as Goodman Brown says goodbye to his wife Faith and sets out for a night in the forest. From the first scene the emphasis is psychological, centered on the ironic relationship between innocent naiveté and the vague, free-floating quality of Goodman's intention:

> "after this one night I'll cling to her skirts and follow her to Heaven."
> With this excellent resolve for the future, Goodman Brown felt himself justified in making more haste on his present evil purpose.

In underestimating what one night's separation can mean, he underestimates the power of time, failing to see the degree to which he has in this domestic parting made himself a particular kind of individual, ultimately the prisoner of his own psychology. For while the story has within it a formal allegory of the loss of faith, the fact of the initial separation, representing as it does the departure from conventional belief, unleashes a social suspension that for him causes all communal relationships henceforth to be determined from within rather than from without.

The middle ⟨sections involves⟩ social fantasies. Goodman Brown's experience in the woods involves projection, and because his basic means of order, his religious system, is absent, the society he was familiar with becomes nightmarish, inducing paranoia. As a third generation Puritan, Brown is historically the victim of an altered relationship to both God and nature, yet what the reader witnesses is the revenge of the id upon the ego, seemingly for the latter's social acquiescence. The people Brown apparently observes in the forest are most real in their absolute reverence for evil and in their complete contempt for naive social beliefs such as his. Under these terms Brown as individual must struggle against society for the very ground of personal value, ever alert for external threats (and everyone is a potential threat), continually betrayed by the double-edged nature (sign and significance) of all social meaning, and periodically forced to declare to himself that his beliefs can only be transcendent: "Look up to Heaven, and resist the Wicked One!"

—Walter Shear, "Cultural Fate and Social Freedom in Three American Short Stories," *Studies in Short Fiction* 29, no. 4 (Fall 1992): pp. 545–46.

⊗

BENJAMIN FRANKLIN V ON THE PURITAN CATECHISM

[Benjamin Franklin V is a professor of English at the University of South Carolina. His works include *Boston Printers, Publishers, and Booksellers: 1640–1800*. In this excerpt, Franklin discusses Brown's un-Puritan view of human nature.]

Without addressing the catechism directly, Colacurcio, in calling Brown "theologically ill-prepared," offers one reason why Brown, before leaving home, has such an un-Puritan view of human nature: perhaps he does not comprehend the tenets of his faith, one important source of which is the catechism. Goody Cloyse might share this view. In terming her former student a "silly fellow," she may intent to suggest that although he memorized the catechism answers, his latitudinarian attitude toward her, Faith, and others before he enters the woods signals his inability truly to understand and psychologically assimilate the full significance of *Milk for Babes*. Even if this is not what she means, the historical record indicates that many young people before, during, and after Brown's time have had difficulty mastering the meaning of a catechism.

This problem attracted the attention of several important seventeenth- and early eighteenth-century divines, both American and English. No less a figure than Richard Mather implies that too many people fail to master the meaning of a catechism. In his 1657 farewell sermon, he observes, "[C]omonly they that fall to erro[ur,] [ar]e defective in the knowledg of Catechistical points." At almost precisely the same time that Brown would have been studying the catechism with Goody Cloyse, however, the English cleric Richard Baxter was suggesting that it is more important for children to memorize the words of a catechism than to understand what the words mean, at least initially. He writes: *"Cause your younger Children to learn the words, though they be not yet capable of understanding the matter. . . .* A child of five or six years old can learn the *words* of a Catechism or Scripture, before they are capable of understanding them." If this attitude prevailed in Salem Village during the time when Goody Cloyse would have been teaching *Milk for Babes,* it might help explain Brown's early inability to embrace the full significance of Cotton's text: there would have been no compelling reason for him to master it; he would have been required only to memorize the words. Yet he would have been expected to understand the catechism as he matured and to begin conducting his life according to its principles. He does neither.

—Benjamin Franklin V, "Goodman Brown and the Puritan Catechism," *ESQ: A Journal of the American Renaissance* 40 (Spring 1994): pp. 73–74.

Plot Summary of
"The Minister's Black Veil"

Hawthorne described "The Minister's Black Veil" as a parable. The story opens outside the meeting house in Milford, Massachusetts, as the sexton pulls the bell-rope and waits with the parishioners for the Reverend Hooper to arrive. Much to the surprise of the sexton and the rest of the congregation, Reverend Hooper walks out of his door wearing a black veil over his face. Goodman Gray, a member of the congregation, suggests that the veiled man is someone other than Reverend Hooper, but it is clear by his figure that it is indeed the minister.

Because of the mystery surrounding this black veil, it does not take long for rumors to surface. Goodman Gray suggests that Reverend Hooper has gone mad. During the service, several people leave because they feel uneasy about the minister's veil. Although Reverend Hooper does not normally have a powerful preaching style, his sermon on this day strikes its listeners as powerfully dark, containing "reference to secret sin."

Later that afternoon, the minister attends a funeral, still adorned in the black veil. The image of the Reverend leaning over the deceased upsets some people at the funeral. When the service ends, some members of the parish remark that they had imagined that "the minister and the maiden's spirit were walking hand in hand."

That evening, Reverend Hooper is scheduled to marry one of the most attractive young couples in Milford. However, what should have been a merry ceremony proves disheartening for both the couple and their guests, because the minister continues to wear the black veil over his face. The bride is noticeably pale and nervous; some guests speculate that the deceased maiden who had been buried earlier that day had risen again to be married by the black-veiled priest. When the ceremony comes to an end, the Reverend raises a glass of wine to toast the couple and spots his reflection in a mirror. Struck by his own frightening appearance, Reverend Hooper spills the wine and runs out of the church.

The Reverend's veil quickly becomes the talk of the town. On the streets and in the homes and businesses, the townspeople wonder about the reason their minister is wearing the black veil. However, though the topic of the veil is on everyone's lips, no one dares to ask Reverend Hooper about it directly. A group of people from the church visits the minister, intending to confront him about the veil, but when they are in Reverend Hooper's presence the black veil is so unsettling that they fail to ask why he has chosen to hide his face.

There is one person in Milford who is not afraid of the black veil: Elizabeth, who is engaged to marry Reverend Hooper. She decides to try and uncover the mystery behind her husband-to-be's hideous veil. She asks him to take away the black veil and explain to her why he is wearing it. The reverend tells her that he can not do either, but begs her to stay with him, assuring her, "It is but a mortal veil—it is not for eternity! Oh! you know not how lonely I am, and how frightened, to be alone behind my black veil. Do not leave me in this miserable obscurity forever!" Elizabeth says that unless he reveals his face and looks her in the eyes, she must leave. Reverend Hooper refuses. As Elizabeth departs, the unhappy minister "smiled to think that only a material emblem had separated him from happiness."

No more attempts are made to uncover the mystery of the veil. It is considered "an eccentric whim, such as often mingles with the sober actions of men otherwise rational, and tinges them all with its own semblance of insanity." Despite the relative acceptance of Reverend Hooper's veil, he remains a frightening creature within the town. Children flee from him, the townsfolk avoid him, and Hooper himself can not stand to gaze in a mirror as he finds his own reflection terrifying.

The black veil does have one positive benefit: Reverend Hooper becomes a powerful clergyman. Sinners feel they can repent in his presence, and he inspires a solemn piety and gloom in those who hear his words. He spends a long life as both a spiritual leader and a public outcast, "irreproachable in outward act, yet shrouded in dismal suspicions; kind and loving, though unloved and dimly feared; a man apart from men, shunned in their health and joy, but ever summoned to their aid in mortal anguish."

When Reverend Hooper reaches the end of his time on earth, he is attended to by Reverend Clark, the minister of nearby Westbury. He is also tended by Elizabeth, who has continued to love Hooper even though she could never bring herself to marry the minister because of his black veil. As the old reverend lies on his deathbed, Reverend Clark suggests that the time has come for him to remove the veil. He reaches down to lift it from Hooper's face, but the minister, with unexpected strength, places his hands over the veil and exclaims that the veil will never be removed, as long as he is on earth.

Surprised, the young Reverend Clark asks what crime is upon Hooper's soul, that he had to wear this horrid cloth. Reverend Hooper replies with a question of his own, asking why everyone is so afraid simply because there is something mysterious about the visible image of his black veil—a symbol of the sins and deeds that are hidden in every human heart. "What, but the mystery which it obscurely typifies, has made this piece of crape so awful? When the friend shows his inmost heart to his friend; the lover to his best beloved; when man does not vainly shrink from the eye of his Creator, loathsomely treasuring up the secret of his sin; then deem me a monster, for the symbol beneath which I have lived, and die! I look around me, and, lo! on every visage a Black Veil!" ❀

List of Characters in
"The Minister's Black Veil"

A decision by *Reverend Hooper* to wear a black veil over his face turns him into a frightening figure in his community. Though he spends his life performing many righteous acts, he is not embraced by anyone. Hooper is buried in his veil, and the image of his mouldering body still shrouded with the black veil continues to haunt the people of the town.

Elizabeth is engaged to marry Reverend Hooper. When he refuses to remove the veil or explain why he is wearing it, she ends the engagement. However, she continues to love Hooper, and nurses him in his final illness.

Reverend Clark is a young and zealous minister from Westbury. When he hears that Reverend Hooper is dying, he sets out to pray by his bedside. He suggests that the veil be removed before his contemporary is laid into the ground, but Reverend Hooper makes it clear that he will be buried along with his veil. ❀

Critical Views on
"The Minister's Black Veil"

JAMES R. MELLOW ON HAWTHORNE'S VEIL

[James R. Mellow is an art and literary critic. His essays and articles have appeared in the *New York Times* and the *Chicago Tribune*. His biography *Charmed Circle: Gertrude Stein and Company* was widely acclaimed. In this excerpt, Mellow discusses the dark secrets that set the minister apart from his fellow men.]

In another story, "The Minister's Black Veil," Hawthorne explores again the secrets of the heart that set a man apart from his neighbors. The Reverend Mr. Hooper, one Sunday, appears before his congregation wearing a black veil over his head. Never an energetic preacher, his discourse on this particular day is on "secret sin, and those sad mysteries which we hide from our nearest and dearest, and would fain conceal from our own consciousness." His delivery on this occasion acquires a dreadful force in the minds of his startled parishioners. The veil, which he has vowed to wear for the remainder of his life, estranges him from the villagers, his congregation, even his intended bride, Elizabeth. He lives "shrouded in dismal suspicions; kind and loving, though unloved, and dimly feared; a man apart from men, shunned in their health and joy." The veil, however, has one salutary effect: it enables the minister to sympathize with every dark affection. "Dying sinners cried aloud for Mr. Hooper, and would not yield their breath till he appeared." On his own deathbed, the minister refuses the efforts of his mourners to remove the veil. "I look around me," he says in his final breath, "and lo! on every visage, a Black Veil!"

It is not without interest that in publishing his odd little tale Hawthorne appended a note saying that the idea for the story had been taken from life. A Reverend Mr. Moody, of York, Maine, had "made himself remarkable by the same eccentricity," Hawthorne claimed. As a young man, the minister had accidentally killed a friend, and "from that day till the hour of his own death, he hid his face from men." The man who is guilty of the death of another—or believes himself to be—is a frequent character in Hawthorne's fiction.

Of equal psychological relevance is the distinction Hawthorne made, in an early notebook entry, between the mask and the veil. Commenting on Emperor Augustus' dying exclamation, "Has it not been well acted?" Hawthorne made a mental note for himself: "An essay on the misery of being always under a masque. A veil may sometimes be needful, but never a masque." He was to speak of his own guarded reserve in similar terms in the preface to *Mosses from an Old Manse.* "So far as I am a man of really individual attributes, I veil my face," he wrote. He was not, he maintained, one of those authors "who serve up their own hearts delicately fried, with brain-sauce, as a tidbit for their beloved public." Yet he was willing to deliver—in the form of his cautious fables, parables, allegories—some of the less palatable truths of the human condition. Like the Reverend Mr. Hooper, Hawthorne had his sympathies with "all dark affections."

—James R. Mellow, *Nathaniel Hawthorne in His Times* (Boston: Houghton Mifflin, 1980): pp. 60–61.

⚘

RICHARD H. BRODHEAD ON HAWTHORNE AND MELVILLE

[Richard H. Brodhead has been a professor of English and chairman of the English Department at Yale University. In this excerpt, Brodhead discusses the structure of the story.]

The figure (in a phrase Melville repeats from Hawthorne) mastered by one Idea, and compelled, by his Idea, to the unswerving execution of an inflexible program, is not, of course, Hawthorne's exclusive invention. The structure of selfhood I describe Melville as imitating from Hawthorne Angus Fletcher finds in all of allegory: Fletcher likens allegory's simplified agents to figures possessed by a daimon, that form of intermediate deity whose effect as it descends on the human self is to narrow it to one function and direct it to one end. The consolidation of the self that Hawthorne's fiction displays is also a standard feature of the gothic—I think of Godwin's Caleb Williams, who slips as easily from having ideas to being had by Ideas as Ethan Brand ("it was but a passing thought. And yet . . . the idea once having occurred to my mind, it was fixed there forever"); or I think of Frankenstein, like Ahab and Chillingworth both agent and victim of an idea that converts wholeness of being into a will for one thing ("one by one the various keys were touched that formed the mechanism of my being; chord after chord was sounded, and soon my mind filled with one thought, one conception, one purpose.") But what Melville marks in Hawthorne is the fusion of monomania as a personality type with a peculiar mode of figuration. In Hawthorne the self recentered within a single faculty sees the world recentered in a parallel way. Its attention fixes on a single object, which it lifts out of the continuum of objects and makes into the sign of its obsession. Aylmer, the perfectionist bridegroom of "The Birthmark," isolates and resignifies Georgiana's facial blemish in this way, projecting his inward preoccupations upon it in such manifold and insistent ways (Hawthorne says that he connects it "with innumerable trains of thought, and modes of feeling") as to convert it into a figure for the sum of his dreads, "the symbol of his wife's liability to sin, sorrow, decay, and death." He is in this the prototype for Hawthorne's idea-possessed men, who in the moment that they succumb to obsession also find an object—Reverend Hooper's black veil, Roderick Elliston's bosom serpent, Arthur Dimmesdale's scarlet letter—in which obsession lodges as an overdetermined meaning. Melville has clearly noticed the conjuction of monomania and figure-making in Hawthorne, because when he recreates Hawthorne's account of the daimonic consolidation of the self in *Moby-Dick*, he insists that its products are a pathology and a metaphor. According to Melville, Ahab's loss of his leg to Moby Dick generates a rage that activates and absorbs every other possible form of human rage until rage is so intense that it achieves a fusion of previously separate things, makes Ahab "*identify* with [the whale], not only all his bodily woes, but all his intellectual and spiritual exasperations." As if still struggling to grasp this notion Melville runs through every way he can think of to say that Ahab's madness is a madness of metaphor: "the White Whale swam before him as the *monomaniac incarnation* of all those malicious agencies which some deep men feel eating in them"; or again: "*deleriously transferring* its idea to the abhorred white whale"; or again: "all evil, to *crazy* Ahab, was visibly *personified*, and made practically assailable in Moby Dick." (my italics)

The curious thing about emblem-makers in Hawthorne is that although it is clear, both to themselves and others, that the meanings they read into their chosen objects originate in an act of obsessive projection, once that projection is completed it takes on an oddly objective and authoritative status. Aylmer selects the birthmark as the symbol for a human condition that he cannot accept, but once he has done so neither Georgiana nor Hawthorne can work free of the notion that this is indeed the birthmark's meaning. Reverend Hooper converts a black veil into the symbol of that secret sin the knowledge of which torments him, but when he presents his neurotic emblem before others it takes on an "awful power"—the power to disclose them to themselves as the secret sinners Hooper claims them to be. Roderick Elliston, the chief case in Hawthorne of what might be called the symbolist as aggressor, thrusts his bosom serpent upon others as their meaning—he "mak[es] his own actual serpent . . . the type of each man's fatal error, or hoarded sin, or unquiet conscience." But the effect of this energetic self-projection is to bring forward the serpent that is them—"by obtruding his own bosom-serpent to the public gaze" he "drag[s] those of decent people from their lurking-places."

—Richard H. Brodhead, *The School of Hawthorne* (New York: Oxford University Press, 1986): pp. 34–36.

William Freedman on the Veil as Symbol

[William Freedman is a professor of English at the University of Haifa in Israel. He has published a book on Laurence Stern and several essays on art and literature. In this excerpt, Freedman discusses the symbolic power of the veil in the story.]

The veil, like the artistic symbol it represents, invites a round of tentative interpretations, all based inevitably on surmise. But its chief significance lies not in these "readings," surely not in its "ultimate meaning," which may or may not be revealed, but in its power to stimulate such efforts and in the still more potent emotional effects it produces in those who behold it. Some of the townspeople are amazed, others awed; some are fearful or intimidated, others perplexed or defensively wise, while yet others are inspired or made hopeful. For all the emphasis on interpretive hypotheses—and there is much—there is as much or more on the accompanying emotional impact. And both, of course, are characteristic of the symbol, the latter more profoundly than the former. Symbols, as D. H. Lawrence remarks, "don't 'mean something.' They stand for units of human *feeling*, human experience. A complex of emotional experience is a symbol. And the power of the symbol," like the power of the minister's veil, "is to arouse the deep emotional self, and the dynamic self, beyond comprehension." The "strangest part of the affair," remarks a physician, "is the effect of this vagary, even on a sober-minded man like myself."

The emphasis on this effect, I believe, reflects Hawthorne's larger concern with the literary symbol as he had begun to employ it in this and other short works. He is preoccupied here with the question of interpretation and effect, tantalized, it seems, by the radiant power of his new instrument. Like ideal readers or critics in relation to a story, the townspeople are obsessed with the veil, intrigued by its possible meanings, overwhelmed by its spiritual and emotive power. Like readers cut off from the author or intimidated by him, "not one ventured to put the plain question to Mr. Hooper, wherefore he did this thing." But eventually, like naive readers unable to control their curiosity and simplistically trustful that the author is the final arbiter of his own meanings (a trust, by the way, that, if we share it, finally reduces the rich tale to the shallowness of the minister's own death-bed fulmination), a few approach him. Futilely, of course, for the creator will not reveal his intentions.

—William Freedman, "The Artist's Symbol and Hawthorne's Veil: 'The Minister's Black Veil' *Resartus," Studies in Short Fiction* 29, no. 3 (Summer 1992): pp. 354–55.

EDGAR A. DRYDEN ON THE STORY AS PARABLE

[Edgar A. Dryden is a professor of English at the University of Arizona and the editor of the *Arizona Quarterly*. He is the author of *Melville's Thematics of Form: The Great Art of Telling the Truth*, and *The Form of American Romance*. In this excerpt, Dryden discusses the distance between the various interpretations of the story.]

The curious relation between the story's subtitle and the footnote that purports to explain it offers a fitting entrance to the shadowy world of "The Minister's Black Veil." In parables as in fables we usually find "'statements of fact, which do not even pretend to be historical, used as vehicles for the exhibition of a general truth.'" And yet Hawthorne asks us to see Mr. Hooper as an historical figure or at least to view him as the literary copy of a historical original whose eccentricity is the source that will partially explain the eccentricity of the fictional character. In the case of Mr. Moody the "import" of the symbolic veil is clear: It is the sign of the shame and guilt he feels at having "accidentally killed a beloved friend." In the case of Mr. Hooper, however, the reasons for his donning the veil remain "unaccountable," and it becomes a "materiel emblem" whose meaning remains to the end obscure. In both cases the crucial relationship is that between figural connotation and literal reference, a relationship that seems clear and uncomplicated in the case of the historical Mr. Moody but aberrant and threatening for the fictional Mr. Hooper, whose life is radically disturbed by the horrible irony that "only a material emblem had separated him from happiness." One could say that the space that separates Reverend Hooper's "simple piece of crape" form the "mystery which it obscurely typifies" is analogous to that which distances the historical Mr. Moody from the fictional character who in some obscure way represents him. This ironic distance is marked in the story by the "faint, sad smile" that "glimmer[s] from [the] obscurity" of the "double fold of crape," a smile that is Hooper's only response to all questions as to his motives for putting it on. And those motives certainly seem obscure. The narrator, like Hooper, offers no specific explanation for the character's unaccountable behavior, although the generic mark inscribed by the story's subtitle suggests that Hooper's actions may have a scriptural or institutional precedent that may be more helpful than the factual one suggested by the footnote. And indeed the Bible seems to suggest several possibilities.

When Moses returns to the children of Israel after spending forty days and forty nights in the presence of God "the skin of his face shone; and they were afraid to come nigh him" (Exodus 34:30) until Moses "put a vail on his face" (Exodus 34:33), a "vail" that he removes when he enters the tabernacle to speak with the Lord. This act of veiling, like that of the Reverend Mr. Hooper, becomes the object of an elaborate figural reading, as in Paul's letters to the Corinthians.

> —Edgar A. Dryden, "Through a Glass Darkly: 'The Minister's Black Veil' as Parable," in *New Essays on Hawthorne's Major Tales*, ed. Millicent Bell (Cambridge: Cambridge University Press, 1993): pp. 134–35.

☙

SAMUEL CHASE COALE ON HOOPER AND THE VEIL

[Samuel Chase Coale is a professor of American Literature at Wheaton College. He is the author of a number of books on American writers including *In Hawthorne's Shadow: American Romance from Melville to Mailer*. In this excerpt, Coale discusses the power of the veil as a literary image.]

Hawthorne himself early on recognized the power of the veil as a literary image. Writing in 1836, in *The American Notebooks*, he mentions "an essay on the misery of being always under a mask. A veil may be needful, but never a mask." Both conceal, but a mask suggests pretense and falsehood, the appropriate object used in disguise. A veil may appear to be more ambiguous, more "needful," since it not only conceals but also suggest protection, ornamentation, a headdress, a covering, and various liturgical cloths. Hooper's choice reflects his vision of himself as a minister in Milford, transfiguring himself into the dreaded icon of his congregation's faith, complete with all its aspects of fear, terror, horror, and fright. And is it any wonder that when Hooper has turned to dust, the thought of the black veil still remains "awful" in the minds and memories of his survivors?

"The Minister's Black Veil" is one of the earliest tales in which this mesmeric process can be shown to take place. It involves both Hooper and his congregation, the desire to read the veil as the specific sign of some specific reason for it, and the experience of gazing upon the veil itself with all the effects that it creates. In the end the veil remains a riddle, creating its own mystery, in much the same way that the people who gaze upon it, as if mesmerized by the spell that it casts, imbue their explanations and emotions with their own sense of mystery and fear. The tale is finally not about the minister but about the veil, and it reenacts a way of seeing, a ritual of gazing, that lies at the heart of Hawthorne's romance.

Most criticism has focused more on Hooper than on the veil. Hooper has been regarded as sinful, almost demonic, faithless, proud, sacrilegious, preoccupied with evil, a misguided religious zealot, a rigid Calvinist, an arch villain, a man afraid of women, a selfish soul fleeing from the darkness of sexuality, a character similar to Hawthorne in Hawthorne's power over his readers, and a living parable who, by rejecting the love that Elizabeth offers him and maintaining his morbid self-possession beneath the veil, not only repeats the very sin he is costuming himself to portray but dooms himself to further isolation and despair. The veil on the other hand has suggested a symbol for mortal ignorance, a false *signum diaboli*, a demonic object to be overcome, a symbol of the failure to communicate, and an object whose effects on the townspeople are such that its very presence vindicates Hooper's behavior. The medium of the tale, the veil itself, has actually been granted the status of an also-ran in the critical history of Hawthorne's story.

—Samuel Chase Coale, *Mesmerism and Hawthorne: Mediums of American Romance* (Tuscaloosa: The University of Alabama Press, 1998): pp. 45–46.

Plot Summary of
"The Maypole of Merry Mount"

"The Maypole of Merry Mount," Hawthorne's tale of a clash between Puritan and Heathen values in New England, opens with a description of the days at Merry Mount, "when the May-Pole was the banner-staff of that gay colony!" There is a mirthful spirit that dwells all year round within Merry Mount. The town is characterized as existing in a joyful, dream-like state, taking few things seriously, be it marriage or death.

The narrative begins on a midsummer eve when the Maypole is being decorated. There is a rainbow-colored silk banner hanging down from the top of the pole, and ribbons, flowers, and wreaths of roses spread throughout its length. The citizens of Merry Mount are adorned in costumes, wearing the antlers of a stag, the head of a wolf, the beard and horns of a goat, and they are dancing with "a real bear of the dark forest," and an Indian hunter. The reader is made aware that there is a band of Puritans watching in the distance. They are mortified by the actions of the Merry Mount colonialists, comparing their masques and foolery "to those devils and ruined souls, with whom their superstition peopled the black wilderness."

This particular festival around the Maypole is centered around a wedding between a young man named Edgar and a fair maiden named Edith. There is an English priest, "canonically dressed, yet decked with flowers, in Heathen fashion," who is present to perform the ceremony. This wedding is the most serious affair that takes place in Merry Mount. The wreath of roses that hangs from the Maypole will be placed over the heads of the newlywed couple following the ceremony, symbolizing their pact of love.

As the priest of Merry Mount begins to speak, the musicians from the colony play an assortment of instruments. Within this collage of sounds, Edgar notices Edith's pensive gaze. Sadness is a crime at Merry Mount, and he asks her what is wrong. She answers that the perpetual mirth which defines Merry Mount has begun to feel ungenuine to her. Edgar admits that he shares her feelings. The acknowledgement of their shared perspective leads them to feel genuine love for one another. "From the moment that they truly loved, they had subjected themselves to earth's doom of care, and sorrow, and troubled joy, and had no more a home at Merry Mount."

It is at this point that the narrative breaks in to inform the reader that the focus will shift from Edgar and Edith. As the town prepares the marriage festivities, the reader is told about the history behind Merry Mount, and the subsequent clash of its merrymaking inhabitants with the Puritan faithful who live nearby. The narrative suggests that the citizens of Merry Mount "would not venture among the sober truths of life, not even to be truly blest." The citizens of Merry Mount hold the Maypole as their greatest symbol, adorning it, gathering around it, and holding festivals to honor it. The colonists of Merry Mount were said to play festive music, sing ballads and tell tales during funerals.

"Unfortunately, there were men in the new world, of a sterner faith than these May-Pole worshipers." These men are the Puritans, who live their lives around the prayer book and the rifle. When they gather, it is "never to keep up the old English mirth, but to hear sermons three hours long, or to proclaim bounties on the heads of wolves and the scalps of Indians." The narrative suggests that the whipping post is the Puritan equivalent to the Maypole. The contrast is simply too great between the two groups and a feud is inevitable, one which will change the complexion of New England.

Following this brief background, the narrative shifts back to the nuptial events taking place around the Maypole. Soon after the sun sets, a group of Puritans storm the gathering. They are led by the Puritan governor, John Endicott. He takes prisoners and cuts down the Maypole. "As it sank, tradition says, the evening sky grew darker, and the woods threw forth a more sombre shadow." He then orders lashings for each of the colonists. He spares the priest, claiming that his punishment will come when he looks in upon himself. Then he commands that the dancing bear be shot through the head, as he suspects him of witchcraft.

When Endicott turns his attention toward Edgar and Edith, he senses their mutual affection for one another. When Edgar asks to take the entirety of the punishment, so as to spare his beloved Edith, Endicott responds by saying that he will not show favor toward his betrothed simply because she is a woman. Edith asks that she be put to death as punishment for both she and Edgar.

Endicott is touched by their youth and their genuine devotion toward one another. He orders them to be taken along with the others, but more gently, as they may make good Puritans one day. He then places the wreath of roses around their heads as a symbol of their passing to a new day, united, in which neither will waste "one regretful thought on the vanities of Merry Mount." ❀

List of Characters in
"The Maypole of Merry Mount"

Edith is the fair maiden who is deemed Lady of the May. It is her marriage ceremony with Edgar that is the central activity around the Maypole. She is the first to question the lack of depth contained within the festivals of Merry Mount. When the Puritans storm the festivities, she asks that she be killed as punishment for both she and Edgar.

Edgar is the young man who is deemed Lord of the May. It is his marriage ceremony with Edith that is the central activity around the Maypole. He inquires about Edith's sadness at the wedding ceremony and discovers that he shares her perspective about the fleeting mirth of Merry Mount. When the Puritans arrive at the Maypole, he asks to take his wife's punishment as well as his own.

The *English Priest* is adorned in canonical clothing as well as flowers and vine leaves. He performs the wedding ceremony which is the central activity around the Maypole. He is spared by John Endicott after the Puritans storm the Maypole. In a footnote to the story, Hawthorn indicates that the priest is a nonconformist Anglican clergyman named William Blackstone, who originally settled in New England but moved to Rhode Island in 1631 after a dispute with the Puritans.

John Endicott is characterized as "the severest Puritan of all who laid the rock foundation of New England." The Puritan governor leads the group that storms the Maypole, and he cuts it down with a sword. He is touched by the selfless actions of Edgar and Edith and orders that they be treated more gently than the other revelers.

Peter Palfrey is a member of the band of Puritans. He is the "ancient," or standard-bearer. ❀

Critical Views on
"The Maypole of Merry Mount"

HARRY LEVIN ON THE SETTING OF THE STORY

[Harry Levin was Chairman of the Division of Modern Languages at Harvard University. His writings include *Contexts of Criticism* and *James Joyce: A Critical Introduction*. In this excerpt, Levin discusses the setting in the story.]

Diplomatic contact with England was to reinforce Hawthorne's sturdy patriotism; but it is already strong in his legendary resurrections of the Massachusetts Bay Colony, where he unreservedly sympathizes with the colonists against the royalists. "The Gray Champion" is his tribute to the independence personified in "the type of New England's hereditary spirit," an indomitable if inexplicable spokesman for liberty, who emerges to announce the overthrow of the Stuarts and will re-emerge in the darkest hours of the American Revolution. The conflict between the Puritans and the Cavaliers, as it is dramatized by the contrast between somber attire and parti-colored raiment, is not so one-sided in "The Maypole of Merrymount." Hawthorne draws upon English folklore and Elizabethan pageantry for his most gayly colorful depiction: a "lightsome couple," garbed as Lord and Lady of the May, and the semi-pagan ceremony by which they are to be married. The tale is darkened, suddenly and ineluctably, by the interruption of John Endicott—the stern iconoclast who tears down the red-cross banner in another tale—along with other "darksome figures" from the Puritan settlement. Darker still is the aspect of depravity they now cast on what before has seemed so naïvely attractive. The maypole is felled, the rebels are dispersed, and order is given that the bride and groom must exchange their rainbow garb for the sober garments of Puritanism. This is their initiation into the mystery that she has sensed—"earth's doom of care and sorrow." But since they must bear it together, they need not repine; their garlanded departure from carefree Merrymount is, like Adam's and Eve's from the garden, a transition from innocence into experience.

"The Maypole of Merrymount," as a literary performance, may well be a *Paradise Lost* in provincial miniature. But Hawthorne, whether through research or instinct, went much farther into the subliminal; he dared to center his graceful parable upon the most primitive archetype of sexuality. By surrounding the maypole with an orgiastic color-scheme, and opposing it with the gloomy denial of color, he balanced the rival claims of Eros and Thanatos, love and death in their universal phase. The compromise implied is an acceptance, specifically, of the institution of marriage, and generally, of the limitations of the human condition. This, despite a certain ambivalence, works to the advantage of the Puritan settlers as against the routed Anglicans. But when the problem is that of religious authority, and the opposition is between the Quaker conscience and the Puritan theocracy, in "The Gentle Boy" Hawthorne sides with the Quakers. Without pretending to share their inner light, he made it the unifying source of his imagery throughout this saint's legend of an infant martyr: "a domesticated sunbeam, brightening moody countenances, and chasing away the gloom from the dark corners . . ." The counter-effect is produced by "Young Goodman Brown," where the emphasis is on "the deep mystery of sin" rather than on the pathos of being sinned against. The pharisaical elders, "a grave and dark-clad company," meting in "the benighted wilderness," are doing the devil's work while professing righteousness. The climax, the passage that incited Melville to his formulation of the power of blackness, is a crisis of faith and an agony of doubt.

> —Harry Levin, *The Power of Blackness* (New York: Alfred A. Knopf, 1958): pp. 52–54.

TERRENCE MARTIN ON CONFLICT IN THE STORY

[Terrence Martin has taught English at Indiana University. His works include *The Instructed Vision: Scottish Common Sense Philosophy and the Origins of American Fiction*. In this excerpt, Martin discusses the clash of events in the story.]

Having undercut the frivolous, carnival-loving Merry Mounters and the stern iron-willed Puritans so that one can identify with neither side, Hawthorne tells us that "the future complexion of New England was involved in this important quarrel." The alternatives, as he presents them, are two: "should the grizzled saints establish their jurisdiction over the gay sinners, then would their spirits darken all the clime, and make it a land of clouded visages, of hard toil, of sermon and psalm, forever. But should the banner-staff of Merry Mount be fortunate, sunshine would break upon the hills, and flowers would beautify the forest, and late posterity do homage to the Maypole." Taken out of context, this passage would certainly seem to indicate a preference for the gaiety of Merry Mount rather than for the gloom of the Puritans. But, we recall, if the Puritans are "most dismal wretches," the Merry Mounters are the "sworn triflers of a lifetime." Furthermore, in this struggle for an empire between "jollity and gloom," there is most immediately at stake the empire of two young hearts, which is, at the moment the Puritans rush forth, in a state of sadness and doubt.

Hawthorne has integrated the elements of his tale by bringing the clash between the Puritans and the Merry Mounters to a climax at the very moment that the true love of Edith and Edgar, now blessed in valid marriage by the Merry Mount priest, has wrought their emotional and moral estrangement. The former Lord and Lady of the May are homeless, subject now to "doom, . . . sorrow, and troubled joy." It is almost as if their graduation from folly has evoked a stern adult world—as if the clash of Puritans and Merry Mounters is an imperial context for their emotional initiation into life. For at twilight, from their hiding place, rush the Puritans, whose "darksome figures were intermixed with the wild shapes of their foes," making the scene a version of the haunted mind—"a picture of the moment, when waking thoughts start up amid the scattered fantasies of a dream." The dream of Merry Mount has ended; Edith and Edgar must now contend with the waking world. Hawthorne has played out the drama of their maturation in the context of tensions inherent in New England history, just as he has played out a drama of New England history in the more intimate context of awakening love.

The somber vision of happiness held out by the end of the tale enforces Hawthorne's moral. Confronted by the love of Edith and

Edgar, even Endicott, "the iron man," is softened; he smiles at the "fair spectacle of early love." With an apparent knowledge of the ever-darkening contours of life, he almost sighs "for the inevitable blight of early hopes." He orders that Edith and Edgar be dressed in more decent attire; he commands that Edgar's hair be cropped "in the true pumpkin-shell fashion." And he lifts the wreath of roses from the Maypole he has destroyed and throws it, "with his own gauntleted hand, over the heads of the Lord and Lady of the May." It was, says Hawthorne,

> a deed of prophecy. As the moral gloom of the world overpowers all systematic gayety, even so was their home of wild mirth made desolate amid the sad forest. They returned to it no more. But as their flowery garland was wreathed of the brightest roses that had grown there, so, in the tie that united them, were intertwined all the purest and best of their early joys. They went heavenward, supporting each other along the difficult path which it was their lot to tread, and never wasted one regretful thought on the vanities of Merry Mount.

—Terrence Martin, *Nathaniel Hawthorne* (Boston: Twayne Publishers, 1983): pp. 79–80.

⊗

JOHN F. BIRK ON MILTON'S INFLUENCE ON THE STORY

[John F. Birk has taught in Europe, the Middle East, and Japan. He has published works on Melville, Faulkner, and Keats. In this excerpt, Birk discusses how the story follows the pattern of two of Milton's poems.]

In terms of key words, settings, and players, then, "Merry Mount" closely follows the pattern of Milton's two poems. "L'Allegro" and the first half of the tale feature like terminologies, call up goddesses of mirth, and evoke rustic sites marked by jovial beasts and stock rustics engaged in *hic et nunc* pagan pleasures. In the same fashion, "Il Penseroso" and the latter half of "Merry Mount" feature the language of gloom; lighthearted social intercourse is quashed by the far sterner termperament bred by overriding sense of Christian duty.

Yet another prominent feature common to Milton's set of companion poems and to "Merry Mount" is the masque, or ritual of revelry. In the former case, the masque appears in "L'Allegro," capping the poem as a dream—"With masque and antique pageantry; / Such sights as youthful poets dream / On summer eves by haunted stream." The corresponding section of Hawthorne's tale exhibits the same. "Never had the Maypole been so gaily decked as at sunset on midsummer eve," we read. The revelers prompt the onlooking Puritans to "compar[e] the masques to those devils and ruined souls with whom their superstition peopled the black wilderness." The resulting raid leaves the "ring of gay masquers . . . disordered and broken," the "Maypole mummeries" disrupted "amid the scattered fantasies of a dream."

Moreover, the chief ingredients in each masque include a sylvan setting marked by music and dance, admittedly in the masque tradition. "To many a youth and many a maid, / Dancing in the checkered shade" of "L'Allegro" finds a parallel in the tale's "Up with your nimble spirits, ye morris-dancers, green men, and glee maidens . . . !" Each case features a musical prodigy:

That Orpheus' self may heave his head
From golden slumber on a bed
Of heaped Elysian flowers, and hear
Such strains as would have won the ear
Of Pluto. . . .

is matched by, "Immediately a prelude of pipe, cithern, and viol, touched with practiced minstrelsy, began to play. . . ."

Each masque also incorporates nuptials. "L'Allegro" refers to "lovely Venus," goddess of love, and then to Hymen, Roman god of marriage, as a participant in the masque. Such passion and fecundity contrast sharply with the "pensive nun" and the "O sad virgin" Melancholy in "Il Penseroso," where but a solitary allusion to marriage—"The story of Cambuscan bold"—is, fittingly, to a nuptial tale left untold. Correspondingly, as the flower-laden priest of Merry Mount prepares to "join in holy matrimony" the "Lord and Lady of the May" as "partners for the dance of life," the bride-to-be at once comes to assume a "pensive glance" called by her lover a "pensive shadow of the mind"—a preview of the imminent "penseroso" half of the tale. These nuptials, too, shall go unaffirmed.

—John F. Birk, "New Roots for 'Merry Mount': Barking up the Wrong Tree?" *Studies in Short Fiction* 28, no. 3 (Summer 1991): pp. 347–48.

[David D. Joplin did his graduate studies at the University of Denver. In this excerpt, Joplin discusses the characteristic mirth in the story.]

Unlike the "heart-easing mirth" in "L'Allegro," which Birk erroneously associates with the revelers' merry making, the Merry Mounters experience a mirth characterized by "jest and delusion, trick and fantasy." It leads to "a wild philosophy of pleasure" that compels them to "play the fool." Such language hardly describes "delights" of "unreproved pleasures free." Rather, Merry Mount's mirth borders on the profane. It is characterized by "erring Thought and perverted Wisdom" that turn people from truth and prudence to a "crowd of vanities." As Sheldon W. Liebman observes, "Clearly, the Merry Mounters . . . live the life of the 'lower man': unrestrained, nonintellectual, and amoral." Quite obviously, Merry Mount mirth is completely opposite to the joy and pleasure that "L'Allegro" celebrates. But it is not so much different from the "vain deluding joys" of "Il Penseroso," which keeps the mind concentrated on "toys" or idle fancies. Therefore, rather than correlating with the pleasures of "L'Allegro," as Birk suggested, the revelers' mirth reflects the destructive vanities of "Il Penseroso."

The Puritan half of the tale finds a similar relationship. Birk states, "As Milton evokes the goddess Melancholy, the emblem here is none other than 'the Puritan of Puritans,' one 'Endicott himself' . . . ." This, however, could not be futher from the truth because Endicott and the Puritans do not match—to use Cleanth Brooks's phrasing—the "melancholy delights" of "Il Penseroso." Indeed, there is nothing delightful, happy, or celebratory about the tale's Puritans. They are stern, "most dismal wretches" who follow ascetic life styles, harshly punishing trifling offenses. Even worse, they hypocritically ignore the humanity implicit in religion by murdering Indians, going so far as to place bounties on Indian scalps. Further, unlike Milton's pensive man, the Puritans are in conflict with their world. They spend their day toiling "through the difficult woods" as they work from sunup to sundown. The story itself centers on the Puritans' violent attack against Merry Mount. In contrast, Milton's *penseroso* is at peace with his world. He does not fight or hate anyone. The only struggle in his life—if it can be called a struggle—is his quest for divine inspiration, as we shall see later. Clearly, the Puritans do not even remotely correlate with the pleasant and dignified character of "Il Penseroso." Any darkness in his world, rather than somber, is "soothing." On the other hand, the Puritan "gloom" and "black shadows" closely match Milton's "loathed Melancholy" born of "blackest midnight." Thus, the Puritans and the revelers both represent negative or destructive forces. Birk did not realize this because he failed to identify the different forms of mirth and melancholy in the poems and the tale.

—David D. Joplin, "'May-Pole of Merry Mount': Hawthorne's 'L'Allegro' and 'Il Penseroso,'" *Studies in Short Fiction* 30, no. 2 (Spring 1993): pp. 187–88.

⊗

MICHAEL J. COLACURCIO ON THE STORY AS ALLEGORY

[Michael J. Colacurcio is a professor of English at the University of California, Los Angeles. He is the author of *New Essays on "The Scarlet Letter."* In this excerpt, Colacurcio speaks on the story's ability to manipulate the reader's expectations.]

"The May-Pole of Merry Mount" is, I should judge, a major tale, but not quite in that full "psychological" sense. It is one of Hawthorne's most richly learned and ironically manipulated stories; and it does mean to speculate, seriously enough, about the relation between original Puritanism and "the future complexion of New England." But its mode is severely mythical; or, rather, demythical. Unlike "Young Goodman Brown" and "The Minister's Black Veil," it cares very little for the personal trauma of its youthful protagonists, who seem more like prescriptive definitions than like "characters." Nobody in the tale is given more than one original thought, to differentiate him (or her) from some archetypal norm; and when that thought does come, almost no attempt is made to make it seem "consistent." This is all quite deliberate, the tale's own law and specific difference; and it requires a certain determined misprision to discover that the Lord and Lady of the May are flat and even a little boring.

What makes "The May-Pole" work so brilliantly is precisely its ability to manipulate our expectations; to make us almost believe that we could have written this pat and patent little "allegory" ourselves—out of our own fund of moral wisdom, if that is what we usually rely on in matters of literary interpretation; or even out of certain "authentic passages from history," if we happen indeed to have read the relevant matter "recorded on the grave pages of our New England annalists." But the tale is absolutely booby-trapped with twice-told ironies, as just a little *more* attention to the quality and condition of the original tellings makes absolutely clear. So that it works to embarrass our more-or-less Puritanic moralism, in even its historicist variety, as thoroughly as it balks our psychologism, itself always more or less Puritanic.

"Puritanism overcomes," we seem to learn, even as in literal fact it once did overcome the only credible challenge to a local hegemony aspiring to become totalized. But how do we know this? Or, supposing we really do *learn* it, why are we so easy to convince? Someone must have our number. But whose vision is this, really? And whose "allegory"? Bradford's, Nathaniel Morton's, Joseph Felt's, Catherine Sedgwick's, Hawthorne's, our own? And who, at this late date, would still be trying to convince us that things were, are, and always will be so? The story itself begs us to ask. It also provides all the clues we need to find the answer. To heed them is to dismantle an entirely factitious (though obviously fairly cogent) allegory of someone else's making and thereby to disarm a moralism that proves as arbitrary as it once was powerful.

And yet, as deconstruction is never the whole story in Hawthorne, a certain burden of thematic meaning survives—moral without being "Puritanic," in the sense in which the example of Endicott teaches us to define that notion; and also political, as we come to realize the fusion of politics and piety in the Puritan world. And that latter point may yet serve as conclusion to both the discussion of this tale and to our whole eclectic chapter. For if Digby has represented, from a political or worldly point of view, the recessive strain of Puritanism, Endicott stands for the dominant. If his excision of a popish symbol from a military banner might be made to symbolize a certain Puritanic nicety of conscience which an otherwise bourgeois revolution seemed yet to require, then perhaps the conditions of honest citizenship demanded the honor of ambivalence. But if his hacking down of the maypole were taken to signify the castration of Nature considered as moral norm, or if his arrest of Blackstone were interpreted as a token of some final triumph over the values of Anglo-Catholic tradition, or if the induction of Edith and Edgar into the pious armies of the Puritan Israel were read as the crucial episode in some anti-Miltonic masterplot, then probably simple protest was much more in order. For unless you could deconstruct those allegories, there might be no more stories to tell.

—Michael J. Colacurcio, *The Province of Piety: Moral History in Hawthorne's Early Tales* (Durham, N.C.: Duke University Press, 1995): pp. 251–53.

Plot Summary of
"Rappaccini's Daughter"

"Rappaccini's Daughter," one of Hawthorne's most studied stories, opens with a fictional narrative digression about the purported author, M. de l'Aubepine (French for Hawthorne), and his obscure place within literary history. The narrative speaks about this author's distinct style ("love of allegory," etc.) and his various volumes of stories (these are actually the titles, in French, of Hawthorne's various works—for example, *Contes deux fois racontées* in English means *Twice-Told Tales*). This narrative digression leads into a commentary on "the ensuing tale," which is supposedly a translation of M. de l'Aubepine's *Beatrice; ou la Belle Empoisonneuse*, recently been published in a French journal.

The tale itself opens with a background description about the primary character in the story, Giovanni Guasconti, and his journey from the southern region of Italy to Padua where he plans to pursue his studies. He takes lodgings in a "gloomy chamber" which had once been a great noble dwelling. In Giovanni's mind, he compares his new home to a place out of Dante's *Inferno*.

Giovanni is met by the old Dame Lisabetta, who is responsible for making his quarters livable. She suggests that if he finds the chamber too gloomy he can stick his head out his window and notice the incredible view he has of the garden below. The garden belongs to the renowned doctor Giacomo Rappaccini, who cultivates unique plants and flowers for medicinal purposes. She mentions that the doctor has a daughter who also spends a considerable portion of time tending the beautiful garden.

Once Lisabetta leaves, Giovanni looks out the window at the garden and notices a particular shrub, "set in a marble vase in the midst of the pool, that bore a profusion of purple blossoms, each of which had the lustre and richness of a gem." As he gazes at the shrub, he hears a rustling in the shadows of the garden and sees an emaciated older man dressed as a scholar, who is quite obviously the doctor. Giovanni is amazed at how carefully he examines each of the plants and flowers in the garden while at the same time maintaining a distance from them. Though he observes these plants at every possible angle, he refrains from touching them or getting too close.

He prunes the leaves in this garden with a protective pair of gloves on and he places a mask over his face when he comes near the purple blossoms in the center of the garden. Yet even with the protective mask, he seems unwilling to spend too much time in their vicinity and ultimately retreats and calls for his daughter, Beatrice, to come to his aid.

Beatrice is a beautiful young woman who has a sibling-like relationship with the flowers. She embraces them and inhales their aroma without a mask or gloves. The doctor tells his daughter that he can no longer care for the purple shrub anymore, as he has already put his life in danger by getting so close. He asks that she take full responsibility for its care. Beatrice accepts the responsibility with great excitement and says that it will be her pleasure to take in the perfumed breath of the pungent flower, referring to it as "the breath of life."

That night, Giovanni dreams of Beatrice and the garden and their mysterious unity. The next morning, he is stunned to find that the garden is as unique and beautiful as he had dreamt.

Later that afternoon, he pays his respects to Signor Pietro Baglioni, a medical professor at the University who had known his father. Giovanni asks him about Dr. Rappaccini, expecting Signor Baglioni to know him as they are both scientists within the same city. Baglioni claims that Dr. Rappaccini "cares infinitely more for science than for mankind." He goes on to say that Rappaccini has been cultivating vegetable poisons because he believes that they possess medicinal virtues. He has even, according to Baglioni, concocted varieties of poisons that are more dangerous than anything nature could create.

The narrative mentions that Giovanni might not have taken Baglioni's words to heart had he been aware of the professional animosity that existed between Baglioni and Rappaccini.

Giovanni says that he must love his daughter more than science. Baglioni says that he has heard that Rappaccini's daughter is learned in the ways of her father's garden and in his experimental medicines. He even suggests that she might be in line to take a position at the university—perhaps the position which Baglioni himself holds.

On Giovanni's walk home he buys a bouquet of flowers and returns to his room. He sits at the window and looks down at the garden below. Beatrice appears from the shadows and walks among the flowers. She approaches the large purple shrub in the center of the garden and embraces it as if it were a sister. Then she plucks a bud from the shrub and, as she's putting it near her heart, a few drops of moisture from the stem drop on an orange lizard. The lizard twitches violently and dies. Giovanni watches in amazement as Beatrice crosses herself and goes about her business. Directly after this incident, an insect flies over Beatrice's head. She looks up in childish amazement before the insect loses its sense of balance and spirals down to the ground. Giovanni is again amazed, wondering whether it had been her breath that had sent the insect to its death. It is at this point that Beatrice becomes aware of Giovanni's presence. Still in a state of shock, Giovanni throws down the bouquet that he had bought and asks her to keep them as a gift. Beatrice thanks him and asks that he accept only her verbal gratitude as she would not be able to reach him with one of her beautiful purple flowers. As she walks back to her home, Giovanni thinks that he sees the bouquet start to wilt.

Giovanni avoids the garden for the next few days, though visions of Beatrice and the scent of the garden instill "a fierce and subtle poison into his system." He is filled with both love and fear for the mysterious and beautiful Beatrice. One day, while walking through the streets of Padua, he is stopped by Baglioni, whom he has avoided since their last conversation. While they are talking, Dr. Rappaccini passes, stopping briefly and staring into Giovanni's face. When he leaves, Baglioni suggests that Dr. Rappaccini is planning to use Giovanni in some sort of experiment. Giovanni breaks away from the intolerable conversation. As he leaves, Baglioni vows not to let him fall prey to the poisonous science of Dr. Rappaccini.

When Giovanni makes it back to his lodgings, he is met by Lisabetta, the housekeeper, who tells him that she can get him into Rappaccini's garden through a private entrance. Though he is somewhat leery, the opportunity is too great for him to pass up. He follows Lisabetta along several obscure passageways to an entrance way that is hidden by the growth of the garden shrubbery.

Giovanni looks around the garden and discovers that the various flowers and plants are mostly unfamiliar to him, with the exception of a few flowers which he knows to be poisonous. As he gazes around the garden, Beatrice emerges. Although Giovanni finds himself at a sudden loss for words, Beatrice greets him with a kind expression. He tells her that he has heard that she is knowledgeable about these various species of plants. She claims that the rumors are false and that her father alone knows about the various breeds of plants and flowers in the garden. As they talk, Giovanni becomes aware of a fragrance which he believes is coming from Beatrice's breath. He is not completely certain whether he is simply smelling the garden or whether it is coming from inside his beautiful companion.

Throughout their conversation, Beatrice and Giovanni walk through the various passageways within the garden, until they end up beside the brilliant purple shrub. Giovanni asks if he might pluck a bud from the bush as Beatrice had promised to give him one the other night. As he reaches for the flower, Beatrice shrieks and clutches his arm. She says that the flower is deadly and that he can not touch it. Then she covers her face and runs out of the garden. Giovanni realizes that Dr. Rappaccini had been watching the entire time.

The following morning, Giovanni feels a burning sensation on his hand. There are purple print marks around his hand, in the exact location where Beatrice had grabbed him. However, it does not take long for him to forget about this strange sting and focus his attention on the lovely Beatrice, with whom he begins engaging in regular meetings. Each day, at the exact same time, he meets her in the garden to talk. He has begun to live for these moments. Though they grow as close as two people can, loving one another in the heart, they never seal their affection with actual contact. Their relationship remains one of words and glances.

One day, Giovanni is greeted in his room by professor Baglioni. Baglioni tells him the story of an Indian prince who sent a beautiful woman as a present for Alexander the Great. What distinguished this woman, beyond her great beauty, was the rich perfume in her breath. Alexander fell in love with her but "a certain sage physician, happening to be present, discovered a terrible secret in regard to her." According to Baglioni, she "had been nourished with poisons from her birth upward, until her whole nature was so imbued with them that she herself had become the deadliest poison in existence."

Giovanni dismisses Baglioni's tale as childish. Baglioni suddenly becomes aware of a unique fragrance within Giovanni's room. He describes it as "faint, but delicious; and yet, after all, by no means agreeable. Were I to breathe it long, methinks it would make me ill." Giovanni accuses him of imagining the fragrance. Baglioni denies his charge and suggests that Rappaccini, who is known to conjure up rich fragrances, is behind it all. He goes on to suggest that Rappaccini's daughter is like a poisonous fragrance. Giovanni requests that his guest stay off the subject of Beatrice. Baglioni claims that he knows her better than Giovanni and that she is as "poisonous as she is beautiful." He goes on to say that the Indian fable which he had recounted earlier has become truth in the form of Rappaccini and Beatrice. He says that Rappaccini would have no qualms about sacrificing his daughter or Giovanni in the name of science. Then he pulls out a beautiful silver vial which contains an antidote capable of countering the most deadly of poisons. He suggests that Giovanni try it out on Beatrice.

Baglioni's visit forces Giovanni to ponder his relationship with Beatrice. He decides that he should devise some sort of test to ease his worried mind. He thinks of the lizard and the insect and the flowers and how each had wilted and died in her presence. He decides to buy the freshest bouquet of flowers. If Beatrice can hold even one flower without it wilting he will be satisfied. He buys the flowers before meeting with Beatrice. On his way to the garden, he gazes into the mirror and admires his stunning features. He feels that he has never looked better, reasoning, also, that the poison supposedly contained within Beatrice has had no effect on him. Then his gaze falls to the bouquet of flowers and he realizes that the flowers, never having left his hand, have begun to wilt. Giovanni turns white and stands motionless, "staring at his own reflection there as at the likeness of something frightful." He thinks about Baglioni's comment concerning the fragrance in his room. He realizes that it must have been his own breath. Then he sees a spider descending from the ceiling. He approaches the insect and breathes deeply upon it, watching as it convulses and dies.

Giovanni heads immediately for the garden, where he meets Beatrice. They walk together through the passageways in the garden until they get to the purple shrub. Upon their arrival at the magnificent yet deadly bush, Giovanni finds himself breathing with incredible ease, savoring each inhalation beside the bright bush. He asks Beatrice where the shrub came from. She answers, with an air of innocence, that her father created it, that it sprang from the soil when she was born. Beatrice then tells Giovanni,

> I . . . was nourished with its breath. It was my sister, and I loved it with a human affection; for, alas!—hast thou not suspected it?—there was an awful doom. . . . the effect of my father's fatal love of science, which estranged me from all society of my kind. Until Heaven sent thee, dearest Giovanni, oh, how lonely was thy poor Beatrice.
>
> "Was it a hard doom?" asked Giovanni, fixing his eyes upon her.
>
> "Only of late have I known how hard it was," answered she tenderly. "Oh, yes; but my heart was torpid, and therefore quiet."

Enraged, Giovanni calls Beatrice "poisonous thing," and blames her for ruining his life by making his nature as deadly as hers. When Beatrice responds by asking for pity from the Holy Virgin, he mockingly suggests that they dip their hands in holy water so they can contaminate every creature that comes after them. To prove his poisonous nature, Giovanni breaths into a swarm of flies, sending the insects spiraling to the ground. Beatrice is struck by the reality of her beloved's condition, claiming that it is the evil of her father's science that has created their condition. She claims that she would never inflict such a thing, telling Giovanni, "though my body is nourished with poison, my spirit is God's creature, and craves love as its daily food."

Giovanni feels remorseful for his outburst. He takes out the silver vial which Baglioni had left him and tells Beatrice that it might not be too late. He suggests that they both drink it and purify themselves together. Beatrice grabs it from her beloved, insisting that she drink it first and that he wait to see the result.

As she drinks the antidote, Rappaccini enters the garden. He approaches his daughter and tells her that she will no longer be alone, as he has arranged for Giovanni to be her bridegroom. Beatrice asks why her father had inflicted such a horrid condition on her. Rappaccini, surprised by the question, answers that he has given her the greatest gift—she is invincible to virtually any power and she has the capability to defeat any enemy. He asks her if she would have preferred to be weak. She answers that she would prefer to have been capable of being loved instead of feared, then sinks down to the ground, dying. The antidote, it turns out, was like a poison to her, and she bids her father and Giovanni goodbye before dying. The story ends as Professor Baglioni looks through a window into the garden and calls out, "in a tone of triumph mixed with horror, to the thunderstruck man of science, 'Rappaccini! Rappaccini! and is this the upshot of your experiment?'" ❀

List of Characters in
"Rappaccini's Daughter"

M. de l'Aubepine is French for Hawthorne. This name is used in the opening of the tale, suggesting that it was M. de l'Aubepine that wrote the story. The description about this fictional author includes a parodied account of Hawthorne's own career and mild insight into the nature of Hawthorne's stories.

Giovanni Guasconti is the primary character in the story. He moves to Padua and takes a room in the old mansion where Rappaccini created his garden. He becomes fascinated by Rappaccini and his daughter, Beatrice. He eventually falls in love with her, despite Baglioni's warnings that she is poisonous. He discovers at the end that he has also become poisonous. This knowledge leads Beatrice to drink the fatal antidote given to Giovanni by Baglioni.

Dame Lisabetta is the housekeeper in the mansion where the story is set. She shows Giovanni the hidden passageway that enters into Rappaccini's garden.

Giacomo Rappaccini is the famous doctor noted for a passion for science that takes precedence over his passion for people. He has spent a life time manufacturing artificial varieties of plants and flowers that produce poisons that might have medicinal value. He raises his daughter on the deadly poisonous breath of a particular purple flower.

Beatrice Rappaccini is the beautiful daughter of Giacomo Rappaccini. She has been raised, since the time of her birth, to breathe the poisonous toxins of an enchanting purple shrub. Her breath is lethal. She falls in love with Giovanni Guasconti and ultimately kills herself when she realizes that her father has infected him with the same poison that has left her isolated from society her entire life.

Pietro Baglioni is a professor of medicine who had been friends with Giovanni's father. He is skeptical of Giacomo Rappaccini's ethics and jealous of his acclaim. He warns Giovanni to stay away from him and his daughter. He tells Giovanni an old Indian fable about a poisonous woman. Ultimately, it is he who gives Giovanni the silver vase filled with the antidote that kills Beatrice. ❈

Critical Views on
"Rappaccini's Daughter"

JAC THARPE ON BEATRICE

[Jac Tharpe was a professor of English at Texas
Technological College. He was a Danforth teacher for two
years and has held various other scholarships. In this
excerpt, Tharpe discusses the character Beatrice
Rappaccini.]

"Rappaccini's Daughter" deals with the enigmatic being of the
daughter of the scientist Rappaccini. The theme is knowledge. The
study of Beatrice occurs within a context broadened by the question
of what Giovanni's perception can reveal of truth, a matter that is
further broadened by the antithesis between empiricism and reason
as represented by the two doctors Rappaccini and Baglioni.
Giovanni may at some point have been intended as the main
character, since he resembles the numerous young men in
Hawthorne's work who are disillusioned by some experience; but his
rôle as it develops in the story is to inscribe point of view, until, near
the end, the author abandons him. Thus, the conflict between
Baglioni and Rappaccini is important in so far as it affects
Giovanni's perception of Beatrice. The fact that he is also an actor in
the affair somewhat complicates his rôle as observer. It means of
course that, as in the case of any observer, what he sees depends
upon what he is. Giovanni is a human actor. He is more involved
than Coverdale and may have served as a warning to him. Giovanni
is even more limited than Coverdale because he is blinded by his lust
for Beatrice. The story displays not the doctrine of isolation that
Hawthorne lamely draws on near the end but the violation of
Beatrice that occurs during the attempt to divine what she is and
subsequently change her, and attempt made by all three male
characters. This is Hawthorne's first real success at showing
characters quite aware of one another, as he briefly did in stories like
"The Birthmark" and "Sylph Etherege," and here, as in those stories
and in the novels, interrelationships lead to violations. Rappaccini
"poisons" Beatrice and Baglioni "cures" her. Both acts are violations
of her essential being. Aside from this, their rôles are confined to
such machinations as Rappaccini may be engaged in and to such

contact as exists between Giovanni and Baglioni. The motives of the two doctors apparently derive to a considerable extent from the two approaches to science. Baglioni represents the Aristotlelian deductive approach that speaks of the "'arcana of medical science.'" Rappacini is the new empiricist. Giovanni and Beatrice are caught in the conflict, wherein Giovanni concentrates more specifically on determining what Beatrice is. He violates her both by the prying and by the attempt to change her.

The themes of knowledge and observation are emphasized in the language by the many words that refer to observation and perception. Light and day are associated with clear thinking. When Giovanni opens the window to look into the garden "which his dreams had made so fertile with mysteries," the sun has "brought everything within the limits of ordinary experience"; except, of course, that he makes a mistake. His fanciful observations in the moonlight had provided him with a truer view. Now his "ordinary experience" of the past has only an adverse effect upon his perceptive ability. In short, and in very earnest, traditional methods of perception, like traditional methods of logic and investigation, are not sufficient. They only generate confusion. Giovanni's conclusion is ironic. "Neither the sickly and thoughtworn Dr. Giacomo Rappaccini, it is true, nor his brilliant daughter, were now visible; so that Giovanni could not determine how much of the singularity which he attributed to both was due to their own qualities and how much to his wonderworking fancy; but he was inclined to take a most rational view of the whole matter."

—Jac Tharpe, *Nathaniel Hawthorne: Identity and Knowledge* (Carbondale: Southern Illinois University Press, 1967): pp. 89–90.

JOHN N. MILLER ON FALSE LEADS IN THE STORY

[John N. Miller is a professor of English at Denison University. He has been a Fulbright Professor of American Literature in Germany. In this excerpt, Miller speaks on the allegorical false leads in the story.]

As Beverly Haviland points out, the false leads in "Rappaccini's Daughter" are numerous and largely allegorical. As a literary construct rather than as troubling combination of floral eroticism and sisterly innocence, Beatrice is overdetermined; she derives from too many literary predecessors, none of whom leads to a clear understanding of her. Not only Dante's Beatrice and Beatrice Cenci lie somewhere behind her, but also the Garden of Eden, Milton, Spenser, Keats, Ovid, and Hoffmann. None of these allegorical allusions, however, clarifies Hawthorne's title character. Instead, Beatrice's numerous literary-allegorical antecedents simply cancel out one another. And although Haviland offers an ingenious explanation for such a tantalizing yet misleading clutter ("Hawthorne used allegory to attack the American version of romantic symbolism, transcendentalism"), it is equally possible that Hawthorne was simply uncertain about and fearful of his allegory. Perhaps its implications were too personal. Perhaps not only Dante's or Shelley's Beatrice, but also his wife Sophia, his two sisters, and even his mother became allegorical models for Signorina Rappaccini.

Hawthorne never seems wholly at ease or consistent with his allegorical Beatrice. Even in the first part of the tale, where Beatrice appears in her most floral guise, a curious tension appears. On the one hand, Giovanni seems to be perceiving Beatrice much as Hawthorne describes her; as viewpoint character, he introduces, intensifies, and perhaps exaggerates his author's allegory, and voices some of the narrator's own judgments. (See, for example, ⟨the sections in which⟩ Giovanni responds with appropriate horror to Rappaccini and Rappaccini's hybrids, respectively.) On the other hand, Hawthorne takes great pains to question Giovanni's perceptions, to render them ambiguous, or to label them as fanciful. Yet while Hawthorne's (or his narrator's) own commentary seems to conflict with Giovanni's fancy, both have the same focus and much the same content.

Consider the following passage, for example:

> Soon there emerged from under a sculptured portal the figure of a young girl, arrayed with as much richness of taste as the most splendid of the flowers . . . and with a bloom so deep and vivid that one shade more would have been too much. She looked redundant with life, health, and energy; all of which attributes were bound down

and compressed, as it were, and girdled tensely, in their luxuriance, by her virgin zone. Yet Giovanni's fancy must have grown morbid, while he looked down into the garden; for the impression which the fair stranger made upon him was as if here were another flower, the human sister of those vegetables ones, as beautiful as they—more beautiful than the richest of them—but still to be touched only with a glove, nor to be approached without a mask.

The first two sentences in this passage seem authorial, with Hawthorne rather than Giovanni describing Beatrice's floral qualities. Then, after the most suggestively erotic clause in the description ("all of which attributes were bound down and compressed, as it were, and girdled tensely, in their luxuriance, by her virgin zone"), Hawthorne projects into Giovanni's "morbid" fancy the female-flower correspondence that he himself seems to have introduced.

—John N. Miller, "Fideism vs. Allegory in 'Rappaccini's Daughter,'" *Nineteenth-Century Literature* 46, no. 2 (September 1991): pp. 226–28.

⊗

RONALD J. NELSON ON SOURCES FOR PIETRO BAGLIONI

[Ronald J. Nelson is a professor of English and Coordinator of Technical Writing at James Madison University. He has published writings on several different authors including Conrad, Piercy, and Cummings. In this excerpt, Nelson speaks on two potential sources for the character Pietro Baglioni.]

I suggest that there were two historical persons named Pietro Baglioni who have been overlooked by previous critics. That their names correspond exactly to that of Hawthorne's creation is sufficient reason to consider them as potential sources. Moreover, what little we know about these two men has some relationship to Hawthorne's Baglioni. In addition, Hawthorne had access at the Boston Anthenaeum to at least three books containing accounts of these two men's lives. Although he did not have borrowing privileges there, Hawthorne spent much time reading at the Athenaeum while serving as editor of the *American Magazine of Useful and Entertaining Knowledge* in early 1836 and later as measurer of coal and salt at the Boston Custom House in 1839–40.

The first of these historical personages is a civil architect named Pietro (Petro) Baglioni (1629–1705), who was born into the famous Baglioni family of Perugia. According to Pascoli, he traveled throughout Italy, France, the Flanders, Holland, and Germany, and had a long residence at Oxford. He published some congratulatory and academic writings of scarce importance on a variety of subjects (*"scrisse in diverse materie varie cose"*) and translated the famous *Use of the Passions* into Italian idiom from the French (*"tradusse il celebre uso delle passioni in idioma Italiano dal Franzese"*). He is, however, to be remembered in particular for his work as an architect in Perugia.

One of his sons, Abbot Alessandro, completed his studies of grammar, rhetoric, and philosophy, and in 1675 gave an erudite oration in the Tuscan language to the press, and in 1677 a few poetic essays in Latin, mentioned by Oldoini. Later, after moving to Rome, he became interested in architecture. Like his father, Alessandro pursued architecture and published works of scarce importance. Another son, Orazio, is described as "very skilled in the literary field and can easily write succinctly, without affectation, and with clarity even in Latin." It is Orazio who wrote the laudatory Latin epitaph for his father and another for his brother Goffredo, both of which are included in the passage, printed as if on tombstones.

Giovanni Battista Vermiglioli's account of the man a century later in *Biografia degli scrittori* (1828–29) covers much of the same material since it is based largely on Pascoli's work, but it does further identify the author of *Use of the Passions* as Giovanni Francesco Senault, the priest who made the Oratorio Translation from the French (Perugia, 1661). The real author hid his name behind the anagram Polibio Tigrane. The other interesting addition by Vermiglioli is that Pietro Baglioni gained a place among the Academics of the Senseless (*"ottenne luogo fra gli Accademici insensati"*), delivering an address in praise of the Ira in the presence of Prelate Rodolfo Acquaviva, Govenor of Perugia. This news was reported by Costanzo Ricci. Mazzuchelli also notes that this man was one of the most illustrious Senseless Academicians of his country (*"uno de' più illustri Accademici Insensati della sua patria"*).

—Ronald J. Nelson, "Two Potential Sources for Pietro Baglioni in Nathaniel Hawthorne's 'Rappaccini's Daughter,'" *Studies in Short Fiction* 28, no. 4 (Fall 1991): pp. 558–59.

⊗

CAROL M. BENSICK ON MODERN INTERPRETATIONS

[Carol M. Bensick is a professor of English at the University of California, Riverside. She is the author of *La Nouvelle Beatrice: Renaissance and Romance in "Rappaccini's Daughter."* In this excerpt, Bensick speaks on the changing interpretation of the story.]

Times have changed. "Rappaccini's Daughter"—long viewed as being "one of the tales by which we measure the greatness of Hawthorne's tales" is now routinely denigrated. It is accused of "artistic confusion," or it is found positively "contradictory." And a recent, denigrating discussion of the tale finds fault with it precisely on the grounds that "topicality" on the one hand, and "Americanness" on the other—just the kinds of things that for a simpler time would have crippled a work with designs on greatness—are *not* there. But what is lack of topicality but universality in time? And what is lack of Americanness but the same in space?

There is another noteworthy way in which times have changed in "Rappaccini" studies. The tale not only looks worse to contemporary eyes; it seems to have a different subject. It used to be a virtual cliché that "Rappaccini's Daughter" was about religion. Now (after a brief interval when it was about interpretation), it is about women in Hawthorne's life (variously his wife, his newborn daughter, his younger sister, an old girlfriend); or it is about stereotypes of women in popular culture; or it is about Hawthorne's uneasiness about virility; or it is about "intercultural romance." In all cases, it is again, as it had been when criticism on it began, and after a considerable spell in which it had become about its themes, about its characters. The new readings are not notably less allegorical than the religious ones; the characters still refer but what they refer to are not ideas but individuals or classes of people.

A further peculiarity of the times in "Rappaccini" criticism is a prevailing disposition to ignore what had formerly seemed objective accomplishments in establishing a context for the tale, the illuminations not of dogma or doctrine but of intellectual history. One would think that the identification of the Transcendentalist–Unitarian "Miracles Controversy" in Jacksonian New England, the "Immortality Controversy" among competing schools of Aristotlelians and between academics and the church in Renaissance Padua, and perhaps of the controversy over medical empiricism in the latter place would have permanently affected readings of the story. These viewpoints the majority of younger commentators, however, simply ignore.

—Carol M. Bensick, "World Lit Hawthorne: Or, Re-Allegorizing 'Rappaccini's Daughter,'" in *New Essays on Hawthorne's Major Tales,* ed. Millicent Bell (Cambridge: Cambridge University Press, 1993): pp. 67–68.

⊛

PATRICIA M. ROGER ON THE PHYSICAL AND THE SPIRITUAL

[Patricia M. Roger has taught English at the University of New Orleans. She has conducted research on American life, Literature and Community. In this excerpt, Roger discusses the story's connection between the physical and spiritual.]

"Rappaccini's Daughter" traces the intricate connections between the physical and spiritual aspects of our experience. The story shows that one's framework for determining meanings—literal and figurative—of things or events powerfully influences one's view of the relations between the physical and spiritual aspects of experience. For example, according to the "spiritual" view of language as expressed by Emerson in *Nature,* the literal meaning of a word refers to its physical meaning, and its figurative meaning expresses a corresponding spiritual, moral, or emotional meaning. This is Giovanni's view of the relations between the literal and figurative meanings of poison.

Giovanni believes that poison corresponds to evil and that health and beauty correspond to goodness, so when Beatrice appears to be poisonous he is bewildered by the disjunction between her apparent health and beauty and her apparently poisonous nature. Giovanni's conflicting feelings and his desire to know whether or not Beatrice is poisonous lead him to think in terms of simple oppositions. He wants to know whether Beatrice is an "angel" or a "demon," "beautiful" or "terrible." Giovanni always works within the framework of oppositions he has set up: either Beatrice is poisonous, and therefore evil, or she is purely good and beautiful, and therefore not poisonous. Hawthorne questions this framework. Beatrice is certainly poisonous; the story provides sufficient evidence for this conclusion in the bouquet of flowers that withers in her hand, the lizard and the insect that she poisons with her breath, and Giovanni himself, who becomes poisonous by contact with Beatrice. The story does not support the idea, however, that her poisonous nature corresponds to a poisonous spirit.

The narrator, toward the end of the story, dismisses the literal, physical poison and advocates understanding "truth" by relying on a kind of spiritual intuition. After Giovanni realizes that he has become poisonous and is furious about it, the narrator reports:

> there came [to Giovanni] . . . recollections of many a holy and passionate outgush of [Beatrice's] heart, when the pure fountain had been unsealed from its depths, and made visible in its transparency to his mental eye; recollections which, had Giovanni known how to estimate them, would have assured him that all this ugly mystery was but an earthly illusion.

This passage, with its Emersonian echoes of transparent truth, shows the tendency of the Transcendentalist position to favor spiritual over material "facts" and to eliminate the role of language in understanding spiritual truth.

—Patricia M. Roger, "Taking a Perspective: Hawthorne's Concept of Language and Nineteenth-Century Language Theory," *Nineteenth-Century Literature* 51, no. 4 (March 1997): pp. 449–50.

ANNA BRICKHOUSE ON THE MEXICAN GENEALOGY OF THE STORY

[Anna Brickhouse is a professor of English at the University of Wisconsin, Eau Claire. She has written on Literary Genealogy and the Politics of Revision in the American Renaissance and the Harlem Renaissance. In this excerpt, Brickhouse comments on the Mexican genealogy of the story, as discussed by Octavio Paz.]

Over a century after the initial publication of Hawthorne's story, the future Nobel laureate Octavio Paz found in "Rappaccini's Daughter" a narrative through which he too appears to "take higher ground" from his nation and its literature. *La hija de Rappaccini,* Paz's only play to date, was first performed on 30 July 1956 in the Teatro del Caballito in Mexico City. A little-discussed part of his oeuvre, the play was included in the series Poesía en voz alta, along with the works of Jean Genet, Eugène Ionesco, and other notable European dramatists. At the time of the play's first performance, Paz had returned to Mexico only three years earlier from a decade-long sojourn abroad (in the United States for two years and then in Europe) during which he had abandoned the explicitly political poetics of his earlier years, befriended André Breton, and begun to propound his own vision of surrealism. Despite Mexican popular demand for a "new 'realism'" that would reflect the country's historical moment, Paz believed that poetry in its ideal form would transcend "the degradation of life, the tyranny of successive time, rationality, ideologies, nationalisms." In the Mexican literary scene of the mid-1950s, which was characterized by intense cultural nationalism, Paz's works often drew heavy criticism for their surrealism, which to their detractors suggested European influence. "Está contaminada por experiencias en otras literaturas" 'They are contaminated by experiences in other literatures,' one critic wrote; "su lírica no pertenece a nuestra tierra" 'his lyrics do not belong to our land.'

It is thus especially fitting that Paz was drawn in this period to "Rappaccini's Daughter"—to an imagined Italy where "actualities would not be so terribly insisted upon, as they are, and must needs be, in America," as Hawthorne wrote in the preface to *The Marble Faun,* the other work he set in Italy. Indeed, both Hawthorne's story and Paz's play take place in hermetically enclosed gardens that seem designed to resist historicization, Edenic spaces that evoke a time-honored literary topos founded on male anxieties about female sexuality. In each text, a young man (Hawthorne's Giovanni, Paz's Juan) becomes infatuated with a tempting woman (Hawthorne's Beatrice, Paz's Beatriz) in a beautiful garden, only to learn that she may destroy him. The particular danger of the Eve figure is her breath, alleged to be fatally toxic, for she has been raised from infancy among the lethal plants cultivated by her father, Rappaccini, a medical scientist of dubious reputation. In each text, Baglioni, a professor of medicine who is Rappaccini's rival, intercedes to warn the young man that the daughter is as dangerous as the botanical realm over which the father presides: for Paz, a garden of "venenos y antídotos" 'venoms and antidotes' that blur the conceptual boundaries between life and death, making them "una y la misma cosa" 'one and the same thing'; for Hawthorne, a garden of plants crossbred to produce "new varieties of poison more horribly deleterious than Nature . . . would ever have plagued the world withal." Seeking to cure the poisonousness of Rappaccini's daughter, the young man administers a potion that promptly kills her. Each author's "Eden of the present world" appears entirely remote from the American hemisphere, unmistakably marked by its author's aspirations to transcend national and historical contingency. The surrealism of Paz's Padua in *La hija de Rappaccini*—located "en cualquier punto eléctrico del espacio y en cualquier fragmento imantado del tiempo" 'in whatever electric point of space and in whatever magnetized fragment of time'—mirrors the self-conscious dislocatedness of Hawthorne's text, which, as the narrator hints, may make "little or no reference either to time or space."

—Anna Brickhouse, "Hawthorne in the Americas: Frances Calderón de la Barca, Octavio Paz, and the Mexican Genealogy of 'Rappaccini's Daughter,'" *PMLA* 113, no. 2 (March 1998): pp. 228–29.

Plot Summary of
"Roger Malvin's Burial"

"Roger Malvin's Burial" opens with an introduction from Hawthorne which speaks of Lovell's Fight, a well-remembered battle that took place in 1725. In his story, Hawthorne tracks two wounded New England soldiers who managed to flee the battle. He claims, in the introduction, that some of the events "will be recognized," as they have been told throughout the years; however, all the names have been changed.

The narrative begins with a description of the sun rising over the trees and the two wounded men resting against the base of an oak. There is a twenty-foot-tall granite rock stretching out above their heads, "not unlike a gigantic gravestone, upon which the veins seemed to form an inscription in forgotten characters." They are resting inside a cluster of oaks, though the area consists primarily of pines. The older man, Roger Malvin, is severely wounded. The youth, Reuben Bourne, is also injured but not as severely.

When Reuben wakes, Roger tells his young companion that he won't be able to travel any further. He says that his wounds are deeper than he had originally thought and he could die at any time. The young boy protests emphatically and tries to convince Roger that together they could make it back. It is clear, however, that not only is Roger Malvin near the end of his life, but also that if Reuben does not make it back soon, he too might die.

Roger has been like a father to Reuben, and he asks the younger man to respect his wishes. He mentions that the granite rock will act as an adequate grave stone. Reuben continues his protests, asking how he would be able to look into Roger's daughter's eyes if he left her father alone in the woods to die. Roger tells Reuben how to relate the details of their plight, going on to offer his blessings for he and Dorcas, his daughter, to get married.

Though Reuben is almost convinced by Roger's sentiment, he still does not feel right about leaving his companion to die alone in the woods. Malvin uses yet another tactic of persuasion, suggesting that if Reuben goes, the younger man might be able to find help for him. The young boy asks his older companion what he might do in a similar situation. Malvin tells him a story about a time when he had left an injured soldier behind to seek help. He says that he came upon a hunting camp and led them to his friend. "He is now a hale and hearty man upon his own farm, far from the frontiers, while I lie wounded here in the depths of the wilderness."

Reuben finally gives in and does his best to make Roger as comfortable as possible. He also climbs to the top of the granite rock and ties his handkerchief to the top of a sapling to alert anyone who might come in search of Malvin. "The handkerchief had been the bandage of a wound upon Reuben's arm; and, as he bound it to the tree, he vowed by the blood that stained it that he would return, either to save his companion's life, or to lay his body in the grave." Reuben then helps Roger sit up against the rock and then he leaves. After walking swiftly through the woods, he turns around one last time and sees his handkerchief waving from atop the young oak, reminding him of his promise.

Reuben's journey home is not an easy one. He meets with foul weather and his body is drained of nearly all its energy. After a few days travel, he collapses beneath a tree. He is discovered by a relief team, which brings him back to the nearest settlement. This turns out to be his own home town.

For several days after his return, Reuben is incapable of responding to any questions about his experience. Meanwhile, Dorcas Malvin sits by his bedside, waiting for him to recover. Finally, Reuben wakes and seems considerably more aware than he had been. When Dorcas asks about her father, Reuben tells her about their travels out of the battlefield, and how they struggled for three days before her father lost the strength to continue. Before he gets into the details, Dorcas concludes that he has died and proceeds to weep. Reuben neglects to tell her that his own will to survive forced him to leave her father alone in the woods to die. While Dorcas weeps, Reuben is too filled with shame to clarify the details. Finally she asks whether he had built an adequate grave for him. He replies that he did what he could and that "there stands a noble tombstone above his head."

Dorcas feels a certain contentment at the thought that her father had received some form of funeral. As time goes on, the town is made aware, through Dorcas' tales, of Reuben's bravery. Reuben suffers "the miserable and humiliating torture of unmerited praise." The couple eventually gets married and Reuben begins a life of internal anguish, having failed to impart the entire truth to his new wife. He can not thwart the feelings of guilt and regret that plague him with haunting regularity. He is unable to shake the feeling that his father-in-law may be "sitting at the foot of the rock, on the withered forest leaves, alive, and awaiting his pledged assistance." As time passes, it becomes increasingly clear that he will have to hide the truth inside, despite the inner voice that is perpetually prompting him to attend to his vow. The weight of this secret makes him irritable and depressed.

Despite having inherited, through marriage, the sizable and well-stocked farm that had once been his father-in-law's, Reuben proves to be a neglectful husband and farmer. His short temper and distracted ways keep him in frequent quarrels with his neighbors, often leading to legal battles. He and Dorcas have a son named Cyrus, who, at fifteen years old, already stands out as an admirable young man. He has proven to be skillful in the forest, both with his feet and with a gun. He strikes many as a future leader on the frontier. Cyrus is as beloved by Reuben as any creature could be, including Dorcas.

In the beginning of May, in Cyrus' fifteenth year, Reuben is forced to sell their belongings and leave town. Dorcas is deeply saddened by the prospect of leaving her friends. Reuben remains quiet, unwilling to acknowledge any regrets, while Cyrus, though shedding a quick tear, is swept away by the thrill of an adventure through the wilderness. He daydreams about leading nations through times of trouble and being remembered as a hero.

The family works though the woods at a healthy pace, living off the game shot by Reuben and Cyrus. Cyrus notices his father's tendency to veer away from the more developed areas. He mentions this to his father, but though Reuben makes some subtle corrections in navigation, he continues to head toward the north, away from the more settled areas.

On the fifth day out in the woods, they make their camp in the middle of a pine forest. Cyrus sets out to find food. Before Reuben heads out, Dorcas mentions that it is the twelfth day of May, approximately eighteen years after her father died. She goes on to mention that she has been comforted many nights knowing that Reuben had been with him. "O, death would have been awful to a solitary man in a wild place like this!" Reuben tells her to pray that they never have to face anything as dreadful and then he sets off into the woods.

Reuben starts out at a rapid pace, settling into a stride as he gets further away from camp. He is lost in reflection, "straying onward rather like a sleep walker than a hunter." Though he walks without heed to direction, he does not stray far from their settlement. He enters into a densely wooded area, comprised primarily by oaks. He wonders if some higher power has led him toward the bones of his father-in-law, so that he might dig a proper grave for him and finally ease his troubled soul. It is at this point that Reuben hears a rustling in the underbrush. He fires on it, "with the instinct of a hunter and the aim of a practiced marksman." There follows a low moan, like that of a wounded animal. As Reuben moves closer he realizes that the thicket into which he fired is next to a gigantic rock that looks like an enormous gravestone. He recognizes the veins "which seemed to be an inscription in forgotten characters." He has found himself in the exact location from where he had fled. The only difference is that the sapling on which he tied his handkerchief has grown into a mature oak; however, the top of the tree, where his banner had been, is bare.

The narrative shifts to Dorcas, soon after her husband and son leave for the hunt. She prepares the area for dinner and gives thanks that she is with people she loves, even though they are deep in the woods. As she straightens up their temporary settlement, she is startled by the sound of a gunshot. She laughs at her temporary fright and feels a sense of pride in the probability that her son has shot a deer. She even calls out his name, but there is no response. She decides to head out into the woods to see if she could lend a hand bringing the animal back to camp. As she walks through the woods, she keeps imagining that she sees Cyrus.

Finally, she sees Reuben in the distance. He is leaning on the butt of his gun and staring at something by his feet. She asks whether he has fallen asleep over the deer. Her husband does not respond. His features are sorrowful and hard. She implores him to speak to her, but he does not seem to hear. Finally he turns around and points at their son, Cyrus, who is lying dead in the forest leaves. Reuben tells her that the granite rock is now a gravestone for both her child and her father. Dorcas shrieks and falls helplessly beside her slain son. Reuben is overcome with emotion. The tears pour out of him "like water from a rock." His sin has now fled from his soul, but at the expense of someone more dear to him than his own self. Then a prayer, "the first for years," emerges from Reuben's mouth, ascending toward Heaven. ❀

List of Characters in
"Roger Malvin's Burial"

Reuben Bourne escapes from "Lovell's Fight" along with Roger Malvin. After traveling for three days and nights, Roger implores Reuben to leave him to die. Reuben promises to return one day to give Roger a proper burial. After returning to town and recovering from his injuries, he marries Roger's daughter, Dorcas, and they have a son. Throughout his life, Reuben is plagued by his promise to help, or to bury, Roger Malvin. When Reuben loses his farm, he takes his family into the wilderness. Some inner force leads Reuben back to where he had left Roger. The story ends after he accidentally shoots his son and discovers the remains of Roger Malvin.

Roger Malvin escapes from "Lovell's Fight" along with Reuben Borne. He is severely injured, however, and tells his youthful companion to leave him to die. He gives Reuben his blessing to marry his daughter. He asks in return that Reuben return to give him a proper burial.

Dorcas Malvin Bourne is the daughter of Roger Malvin. She marries Reuben Bourne and they have a son, Cyrus. She does not know that Reuben had left her father to die alone in the woods. The story ends after she discovers her husband leaning over the dead body of her son. She shrieks and falls to her knees in despair.

Cyrus Bourne is the son of Reuben and Dorcas Bourne. He is known as a skillful hunter, even at his young age. He is fifteen years old when he and his family head out into the woods. His father accidentally shoots him dead when they are both hunting for dinner. ❀

Critical Views on
"Roger Malvin's Burial"

PATRICIA ANNE CARLSON ON SETTING AND
INTERPRETATION

[Patricia Anne Carlson has taught English at Rose-Hulman
Institute of Technology in Terre Haute, Indiana. Her works
include *Hawthorne's Functional Settings: A Study of Artistic
Method*. In this excerpt, Carlson speaks on the many levels
of interpretation within the story.]

"Roger Malvin's Burial" is one of the earliest and, at the same time,
one of the most complex of the major tales. ⟨. . .⟩ The richness of its
thematic content is suggested by H. H. Waggoner's remarks about
the tale and its conclusion.

> These closing words of the story, like the Biblical allusions
> throughout, make it clear that a reading of the tale in terms of both
> primitive religious myth and the historical and theological aspects of
> creedal Christianity are as clearly justified as the psychological reading
> is. Oedipus and the sacrificial savior loom in the background of this
> tale whose foreground is fashioned out of colonial history and the
> nature and effects of concealed guilt. Original Sin and the Atonement
> are as clearly involved in Reuben Bourne's story, as are the psychology
> of guilt and the demands of the unconscious.

Such multiplicity of interpretative level makes an essentially
monolithic examination (which the nature of this study demands)
appear unsatisfying and simplistic. Nevertheless, the functional
setting is efficacious in all facets of the tale, and, because of this
pervasiveness, has a certain authority and autonomy which justifies
its being considered without constant reference to the "pagan-
Christian-historical-theological-psychological" amalgamation of its
theme.

One of the best examinations, to date, of the scenic properties as
functional components of "Roger Malvin's Burial" is Virginia O.
Birdsall's "Hawthorne's Oak Tree Image," which analyzes the oak tree
as the locus for horizontal unification of the dramatic-narrative
structure as well as for vertical unification of the levels of meaning.
Though brief, Ms. Birdsall's article gives a wealth of interpretive

insight—far too much to be adequately recounted here. Her findings, nevertheless, support this study. She says that the "tree functions most obviously . . . in unifying the tale on the level of direct action. Here it is simply a tree—a natural phenomenon rooted at that point in the forest where the narrative action begins, later useful to Reuben as a marker, and at the end of the narrative, still rooted at the same spot." As the story progresses—Ms. Birdsall notes—the author loads the image with mythic, religious, and psychological implication. "The fact that Hawthorne insistently makes the tree an oak and not one of 'the pines which were the usual growth of the land'" is very significant; "historically and mythologically, the oak has always been a symbol of strength. . . ." Furthermore, as the tale evolves it becomes "apparent how intimately the oake tree is tied in with the rest of the tale's complex Biblical allusion." Finally, the oak is an objective correlative for the physical and the psychological character of Reuben. When the youth ties the bloody rag to the branch, he interlocks the destiny of the tree with that of his own life. Eighteen years later, as the very moment of Reuben's expiation "the withered top-most bough of the oak loosen[s] itself in the stilly air, and [falls] in soft, light fragments upon the rock, upon the leaves, upon Reuben, upon his wife and child, and upon Roger Malvin's bones" in an anthropomorphic gesture of blessing. This correlation is carried out not only in the action but also in the verbal texture of Hawthorne's parallel descriptions of Reuben and the oak. As Ms. Birdsall comments, "like himself, it [the tree] was introduced into the tale as 'a young and vigorous sapling,' and like Reuben, it has grown and changed—has become an older tree, although far, indeed, from its maturity."

—Patricia Anne Carlson, *Hawthorne's Functional Settings: A Study of Artistic Method* (Amsterdam: Editions Rodopi N.V., 1977): pp. 153–54.

[Shifra Hochberg has taught at Bar Ilan University in Israel. She is the author of articles on Dickens and George Eliot. In this excerpt, Hochberg discusses the nomenclature used in the story.]

The journey imagery of Roger's dying words leads us to a final, related point about nomenclature in the literal meaning of Reuben's surname. Unlike the given names in the tale, "bourne" is a word that would not require etymological exegesis for the educated reader, and its meaning as a "destination"—not merely as a "stream" or a "limit"—is significant in light of the story's pervasive journey imagery, which has been overlooked by critics. Roger's final blessing—"my dying eyes can see a long and pleasant path in which you will journey together"—comments ironically on the circularity of Reuben's "solitary pilgrimage." As Hawthorne writes, "His steps were imperceptibly led almost in a circle"—literally around the vicinity of the campsite, but also back to the spot where Roger had expired. This journey motif is even more dramatically described in a passage which conflates it with the other meaning of "bourne" as "limit" and highlights the historical dimensions of the tale:

> O, who, in the enthusiasm of a daydream, has not wished that he were a *wanderer* in a world of summer wilderness, with one fair and gentle being hanging lightly on his arm? In youth his free and exulting step would know no *barrier* . . . ; and when hoary age, after long, long years of that pure life, stole on and found him there, it would find him *the father of a race, the patriarch of a people, the founder of a mighty nation yet to be.* (emphasis added)

This rhapsody is not only descriptive of a peregrination in a "post-paradisical wilderness where there is guilt and blood sacrifice" and where the American Adam must die because Eden is corrupt, as Donohue proposes. In view of the meaning of Reuben's surname, it likewise comments on the circular journey which climaxes in the death of Cyrus, thereby cutting Reuben off from the historical future and from the continuity of the frontier experience. Indeed, as Hawthorne tells us in a passage replete with irony, "all who anticipated the return of Indian war spoke of Cyrus Bourne as a future leader in the land."

The historicity of the tale, expressed in Reuben's isolation from the collective destiny of America, is likewise alluded to in the Biblical imagery of his tears, which "gushed out like water from a rock" as he weeps over the body of Cyrus. Unlike Thompson, who sees this as a reference to Isaiah 48:21, I suggest that it also—and more significantly—alludes to Numbers 20:11–12, where Moses countermands God's wishes, striking the rock to produce water rather than speaking to it, and is, in consequence, forever barred entry into the Promised Land.

Thus we find that names in "Roger Malvin's Burial," both in their more abstruse etymological derivations and in their more obvious literal denotations, serve as plot pointers or echoes and as adjuncts to the creation of theme, image, and textual irony. A reading of the story along these lines neither contradicts nor negates past critical exegesis, but instead, further illuminates the rich texture of the tale. It shows that at the heart of Hawthorne's fictional art lies the simple meaning, from which all else derives.

—Shifra Hochberg, "Etymology and the Significance of Names in 'Roger Malvin's Burial,'" *Studies in Short Fiction* 26, no. 3 (Summer 1989): pp. 320–21.

G. R. THOMPSON ON STRATEGIES OF NARRATIVE INTERVENTION

[G. R. Thompson is a professor of English at Purdue University. His works include *Poe's Fiction: Romantic Irony in the Gothic Tales* and *Romantic Arabesque, Contemporary Theory and Postmodernism.* In this excerpt, Thompson speaks on the pattern of narrative intrusion in the story.]

After the opening paragraph, the tale proper begins, indicated by spaced periods across the page (or in some editions white space). There are four such indications of sections in the narrative and, in different degrees, four additional main intrusions by the narrator, framing the tale symmetrically around five narrative intrusions and five episodes.

Following the hints of the historical frame, the overt themes of the tale involve concepts of fate and fatality. It is the ironic fate of Reuben Bourne to suffer excruciating guilt over something for which he is essentially blameless and to attribute to a supernatural fate his inner psychological anguish. The implied general reader (as normative narratee) is faced with a discrepancy between Reuben's view of the "commandment" laid upon him (whether perceived culturally or individually) and a commonsense assessment of the particular situation within the general situation (the problem of remaining by the side of his dying comrade in the face of the rapid approach of an Indian war party). The tale is suffused with a sense of supernatural fatality, but it is simultaneously a psychological study of obsessive guilt working on the subconscious mind. In this double structure, the two narratives of "Roger Malvin's Burial" are rather obvious. The narratological semiotics—not of the function of the narrator, but of the narratee—constitute a major variation on those of the second half of "The Gray Champion." At the precise mid-point of the narrative after Reuben has told his gray lie to Dorcas about the burial ("I did what I could") and equivocated ("there stands a noble tombstone above his head": that is, the tall rock under which he had left Malvin), the narrator summarizes Reuben's feelings of guilt and hypocrisy, especially "the miserable and humiliating torture of unmerited praise." Reuben's problem is intensified when his neighbors all acknowledge his worthiness to "the hand of the fair maiden to whose father he had been 'faithful unto death.'" It is here that the narrator inserts, as though in the understated ironic mode of a Jane Austen narrator: ". . . as my tale is not of love, it shall suffice to say that in the space of a few months Reuben became the husband of Dorcas Malvin."

Reuben's mind is at this point assaulted by what the narrator calls "an incommunicable thought," something he is self-compelled to conceal "from her whom he most loved and trusted." "Pride, the fear of losing her affection, the dread of universal scorn, forbade him to rectify this falsehood." Although at this time he feels that he deserves no censure for leaving Malvin, "concealment had imparted to a justifiable act much of the secret effect of guilt; and Reuben, while reason told him that he had done right, experienced in no small degree the mental horrors which punish the perpetrator of undiscovered crime. By a certain association of ideas, he at times almost imagined himself a murderer." For years afterward, Reuben is haunted by a "torturing fancy that his father-in-law was yet sitting at the foot of the rock, on the withered forest leaves, alive, and awaiting his pledged assistance."

These "mental deceptions" come and go, and though he never "mistake[s] them for realities," he is yet "conscious that he had a deep vow unredeemed, and that an unburied corpse was calling to him out of the wilderness." Both the idea of "redemption" (in this case as the unredeemed) and "wilderness" have taken on several meanings. For one thing, if Reuben for a moment admits what really happened, he is truly in a wilderness. In the narrator's opinion, then, there are two levels of delusion, ironically related. One (Malvin sitting by the rock waiting) is a mental delusion, that is, not literally real; the second (the moral vow to the unburied) is of ambiguous status. The second is not one that Reuben Bourne can see as illusory (as he can the first) or as of no legitimate moral force; instead, he is imprisoned by or within it. The first is literally unreal; the second, as the narrator knows, is unrealistic in another way. Reuben's wilderness experience is ontological as well as moral.

—G. R. Thompson, *The Art of Authorial Presence: Hawthorne's Provincial Tales* (Durham, N.C.: Duke University Press, 1993): pp. 97–98.

MICHAEL J. COLACURCIO ON REUBEN BOURNE'S LOGIC

[Michael J. Colacurcio is a professor of English at the University of California, Los Angeles. He is the author of *The Province of Piety: Moral History in Hawthorne's Early Tales*. In this excerpt, Colacurcio discusses the logic that drives the story.]

Yet the logic of "Roger Malvin's Burial" may offer an even more severe education in the competing claims of general principle and historical circumstance. It is, on one hand, the tale most boldly claimed by the psychoanalytic science of Frederick Crews; and indeed the experience of its protagonist seems compulsed and nightmarish even after Crews has recanted his systematic

Freudianism. On the other hand, however, it attaches itself to an event far more obscure than the American Revolution or even the Salem Witchcraft. For—apart from the tale's own headnote—what modern reader has even *heard* of "Lovell's Fight"?

Innocent of all such concerns, Crews opposed instead certain orthodox approaches to the case of Reuben Bourne: Unless one were extremely wary about the ending of this disturbing tale, one had better not venture a religious interpretation at all. What happens there is more barbarous than pious or at any rate, more psychologically elemental than rationally moral. Reuben Bourne may feel that "his sin was expiated" in the killing of his son, but (unless one posits a "teleological suspension of the ethical") the issue is not salvation but psychic survival. The plot of which is clear enough: Ineffectually remorseful ever since his abandonment of his prospective father-in-law, Reuben has thwarted himself in business, poisoned his social relations, then wandered compulsively back to the spot where it all began, to expiate in slaughter what began in grief. Obscurely guilty of the death of a figurative father, he frees his tormented soul by killing—not *quite* accidentally—his literal son. "Regeneration Through Violence" with a vengeance.

Chastened, the moralist may protest that it requires less than oedipal theory to notice that Reuben will suffer great distress at the decision he seems forced to make: Heroically, he would like to remain beside his dying companion in arms; as a Christian, perhaps, he would like to "lay down his life for his friend"; yet he is utilitarian enough to realize the greatest good of the greatest number; and he *would* like to save his own skin. He sees at once the truth of Malvin's prediction: Dorcas will be upset at first, but she will come around; things will be awkward in the meantime, but they must be endured. Yet it is this very meantime that Reuben fears he cannot endure: He knows that Dorcas's eyes, if not her voice, will accuse him of cowardice; and he cannot face this refracted version of himself. This is why he allows a tough and ruefully smiling Malvin to persuade him that his real project is to go off and seek a means of rescue. Only thus can he save his life and still maintain the standard of heroism objectified in the glance of Dorcas.

Clearly, this old-fashioned psychology is as relevant as Freud. Source critics might even observe that Reuben's moral dilemma is constructed as a traditional "case of conscience," the very sort of problem treated in one of Hawthorne's favorite seventeenth-century authors. Indeed this older style of motive analysis—pressing rational analysis to the point of disappearance—may even explain why Reuben feels guilty in the first place: not for refusing "the gratuitous sacrifice of his own life," but for "concealment," of both fact and motive, from all concerned. Including himself.

—Michael J. Colacurcio, "'Certain Circumstances': Hawthorne and the Interest of History," in *New Essays on Hawthorne's Major Tales*, ed. Millicent Bell (Cambridge: Cambridge University Press, 1993): pp. 45–46.

⊛

NANCY BUNGE ON THE THEME OF THE STORY

[Nancy Bunge is a professor in the Department of American Thought and Language at Michigan State University. She has published literary analyses of American writers in journals such as *The Nathaniel Hawthorne Journal, Studies in Short Fiction*, and *The Walt Whitman Review*. In this excerpt, Bunge speaks on the consistency of theme within the story.]

"Roger Malvin's Burial" shows that violating one's heart to obey convention can hurt others as well as oneself. Stranded in the woods with his mortally wounded future father-in-law, Roger Malvin, Reuben Bourne must decide whether to stay and perish with Roger or try to save himself by leaving. His father-in-law urges him to go, but asks Roger to return and bury his corpse. The narrator explains this request: "An almost superstitious regard . . . was paid by the frontier inhabitants to the rites of sepulture; and there are many instances of the sacrifice of life, in the attempt to bury those who had fallen by the 'sword of the wilderness.'" Roger promises and leaves, although reluctantly, because he wants to live: "His generous nature would fain have delayed him, at whatever risk, till the dying scene were past; but the desire of existence, and the hope of happiness had strengthened in his heart, and he was unable to resist them."

When Roger returns home, he tells his future wife, Dorcas, of her father's death. She immediately asks if he buried her father. The narrator describes this as "the question by which her filial piety manifested itself"; Dorcas automatically translates feelings into group norms. Reuben fears losing her if he tells the truth, so he says: "My hands were weak, but I did what I could . . . There stands a noble tomb-stone above his head, and I would to Heaven I slept as soundly as he!" Then Reuben begins to feel guilty, not for leaving Roger, but because "concealment had imparted to a justifiable act, much of the secret effect of guilt."

Although Reuben's dishonesty preserves his relationship to Dorcas and his stature in the community, guilt destroys his life. Miserable with himself, he behaves miserably to others. He loves only his son, Cyrus, "as if whatever was good and happy in his own nature had been transferred to his child, carrying his affections with it." When bankruptcy drives him from town, he sets out with Dorcas and Cyrus. As they travel to a new life, Reuben strays from his route; his guilt unconsciously pulls him to the place he left Roger Malvin. Reuben accepts this diversion because "he trusted that it was Heaven's intent to afford him an opportunity of expiating his sin."

As they journey through the woods, Reuben hears a noise, shoots, and discovers that he has killed his son in the same place he left Roger Malvin to die. When Dorcas investigates the noise, Reuben confesses the truth to her. At that moment, he becomes, once more, a feeling human being: "Then Reuben's heart was stricken, and the tears gushed out like water from a rock." Reuben can now pray: "the vow that the wounded youth had made, the blighted man had come to redeem. His sin was expiated, the curse was gone from him; and, in the hour, when he had shed blood dearer to him than his own, a prayer, the first for years, went up to Heaven from the lips of Reuben Bourne." Some critics accept the narrator's apparent judgement here: Reuben redeems his life by killing his son. Others proclaim Reuben's salvation a psychological delusion, offering diverse explanations of his error. The view of the second group seems more consistent with the whole tale.

—Nancy Bunge, *Nathaniel Hawthorne: A Study of the Short Fiction* (New York: Twayne Publishers, 1993): pp. 14–15.

Works by
Nathaniel Hawthorne

Fanshawe: A Tale. 1828.

Twice-Told Tales. 1837.

Grandfather's Chair. 1841.

Famous Old People. 1841.

Liberty Tree. 1841.

Twice-Told Tales (second edition). 1842.

Biographical Stories for Children. 1842.

Mosses from an Old Manse. 1846. (rev. 1854)

The Scarlet Letter. 1850.

The House of the Seven Gables. 1851.

The Snow-Image and Other Twice-Told Tales. 1851.

True Stories from History and Biography. 1851.

A Wonder-Book for Girls and Boys. 1852.

The Life of Franklin Pierce. 1852.

The Blithedale Romance. 1852.

Tanglewood Tales for Girls and Boys. 1853.

The Marble Faun. 1860.

Our Old Home. 1863.

Passages from the American Notebooks. 1868.

Passages from the English Notebooks. 1870.

Passages from the French and Italian Notebooks. 1871.

Septimius Felton. 1872.

The Dolliver Romance. 1876.

Dr. Grimshawe's Secret. 1883.

The Ancestral Footstep. 1883.

Works about
Nathaniel Hawthorne

Adkins, Nelson F. "The Early Projected Works of Nathaniel Hawthorne," *Papers of the Bibliographical Society of America* (1945): pp. 119–55.

Arvin, Newton. *Hawthorne*. Boston: Little, Brown, 1929.

Baym, Nina. *The Shape of Hawthorne's Career*. Ithaca, N.Y.: Cornell University Press, 1976.

Bell, Michael Davitt. *Hawthorne and the Historical Romance of New England*. Princeton, N.J.: Princeton University Press, 1971.

Benswick, Carol Marie. *La Nouvelle Beatrice: Renaissance and Romance in "Rappaccini's Daughter."* New Brunswick: Rutgers University Press, 1985.

Berlant, Lauren. *The Anatomy of National Fantasy*. Chicago: University of Chicago Press, 1991.

Brodhead, Richard H. *The School of Hawthorne*. New York: Oxford University Press, 1986.

Cagidemetrio, Alide. *Fictions of the Past: Hawthorne and Melville*. Amherst: University of Massachusetts Press, 1992.

Colacurcio, Michael J. *The Province of Piety: Moral History in Hawthorne's Early Tales*. Cambridge, Mass.: Harvard University Press, 1984.

Crews, Frederick. *The Sins of the Fathers: Hawthorne's Psychological Themes*. New York: Oxford University Press, 1966.

Daly, Robert J. "History and Chivalric Myth in 'Roger Malvin's Burial,'" *Essex Institute Historical Collections* 109 (1973): pp. 99–115.

Doubleday, Neal Frank. *Hawthorne's Early Tales: A Critical Study*. Durham, N.C.: Duke University Press, 1972.

Dryden, Edgar A. *Nathaniel Hawthorne: The Poetics of Enchantment*. Ithaca, N.Y.: Cornell University Press, 1977.

Erlich, Gloria. *Family Themes and Hawthorne's Fiction*. New Brunswick, N.J.: Rutgers University Press, 1984.

Feidelson, Charles. *Symbolism in American Literature*. Chicago: University of Chicago Press, 1953.

Fogle, Richard Harter. *Hawthorne's Fiction: The Light and the Dark*. Norman: University of Oklahoma Press, 1964.

Gollin, Rita K. *Nathaniel Hawthorne and the Truth of Dreams*. Baton Rouge: Louisiana State University Press, 1979.

Hall, Lawrence Sargeant. *Hawthorne: Critic of Society*. New Haven, Conn.: Yale University Press, 1944.

Hawthorne, Julian. *Nathaniel Hawthorne and His Wife*, 2 Vols. Boston: J. R. Osgood, 1884.

Hoffman, Daniel C. *Form and Fable in American Fiction*. New York: Oxford University Press, 1961.

Jacobson, Richard J. *Hawthorne's Conception of the Creative Process*. Cambridge, Mass.: Harvard University Press, 1965.

James, Henry. *Hawthorne*. London: Macmillan, 1879.

Kesselring, M. L. *Hawthorne's Reading, 1828–1850*. New York: New York Public Library, 1949.

Lathrop, George P. *A Study of Hawthorne*. Boston: J. R. Osgood, 1876.

Long, Robert Emmet. *The Great Succession: Henry James and the Legacy of Hawthorne*. Pittsburgh: University of Pittsburgh Press, 1979.

Marks, Alfred H. "German Romantic Irony in Hawthorne's Tales," *Symposium* 7 (1953): 274–305.

Miller, J. Hillis. *Hawthorne and History: Defacing It*. Cambridge, Mass.: Basil Blackwell, 1991.

Newberry, Frederick. *Hawthorne's Divided Loyalties: England and America in His Works*. Rutherford, N.Y.: Fairleigh Dickinson University Press, 1989.

Newman, Lea Bertani Vozar. *A Reader's Guide to the Short Stories of Nathaniel Hawthorne*. Boston: G. K. Hall, 1979.

Person, Leland S., Jr. *Aesthetic Headaches: Women and Masculine Poetics in Poe, Melville, and Hawthorne*. Athens: University of Georgia Press, 1988.

Pfister, Joel. *The Production of Personal Life: Class, Gender and the Psychological in Hawthorne's Fiction*. Stanford, Calif.: Stanford University Press, 1991.

Shaw, Peter. *American Patriots and the Rituals of Revolution*. Cambridge, Mass.: Harvard University Press, 1981.

Simpson, Lewis P. "John Adama and Hawthorne: The Fiction of the Real American Revolution," *Studies in the Literary Imagination* 9 (1976): pp. 1–18.

Stein, William Bysshe. *Hawthorne's Faust: A Study of the Devil Archetype.* Gainesville: University of Florida Press, 1953.

Stoer, Taylor. *Hawthorne's Mad Scientists: Pseudoscience and Social Science.* Hamden, Conn: Archon Books, 1978.

Swann, Charles. *Nathaniel Hawthorne: Tradition and Revolution.* Cambridge, Mass.: Harvard University Press, 1991.

Waggoner, Hyatt H. *Hawthorne: A Critical Study.* Cambridge: Harvard University Press, 1955.

Warren, Robert Penn. "Hawthorne Revisited: Some Remarks on Hell-firedness," *Sewanee Review* 81 (1973): pp. 75–111.

Index of
Themes and Ideas